Calvin Coolidge
At Home in Northampton

Susan Lewis Well

The profits on the sales of this book will support the
CALVIN COOLIDGE PRESIDENTIAL LIBRARY AND MUSEUM
Forbes Library, 20 West Street, Northampton, MA 01060

Published by the Calvin Coolidge Presidential Library and Museum
Forbes Library, 20 West Street, Northampton, MA 01060

Printed by Collective Copies, 93 Main Street, Florence, MA 01062
& 71 South Pleasant Street, Amherst, MA 01002
Design and Layout by Steve Strimer
Map by Lisa Carta, Image and Design

©2008 Susan Lewis Well
All Rights Reserved

ISBN 0-9600828-7-5

For Arnie

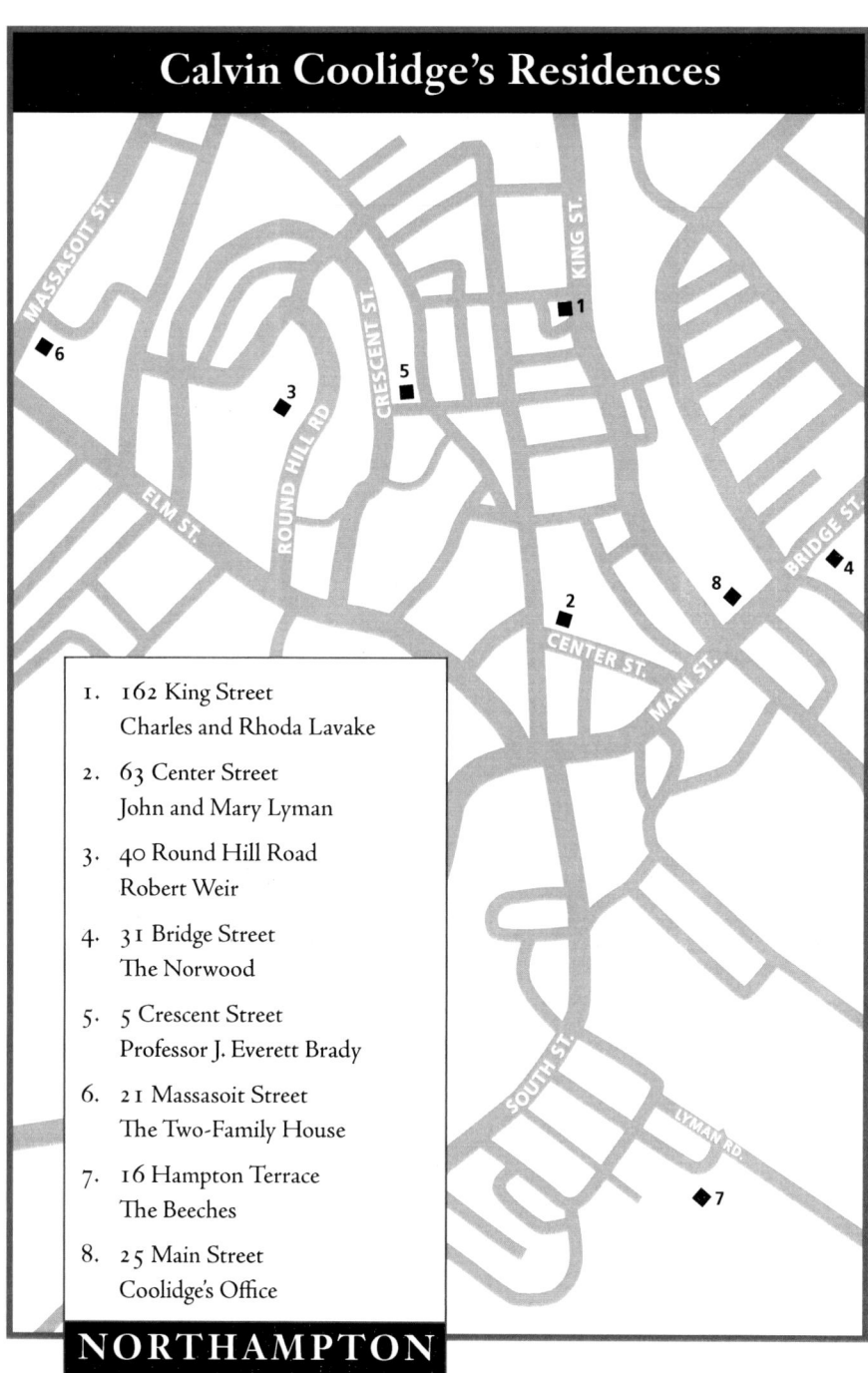

Calvin Coolidge's Residences

1. 162 King Street
   Charles and Rhoda Lavake

2. 63 Center Street
   John and Mary Lyman

3. 40 Round Hill Road
   Robert Weir

4. 31 Bridge Street
   The Norwood

5. 5 Crescent Street
   Professor J. Everett Brady

6. 21 Massasoit Street
   The Two-Family House

7. 16 Hampton Terrace
   The Beeches

8. 25 Main Street
   Coolidge's Office

NORTHAMPTON

The buildings that still exist are private residences.
Please respect the rights and privacy of the present owners.

Table of Contents

Map v

Acknowledgments ix

Chronology of Coolidge's Life and Homes in Northampton, Massachusetts xi

Preface xiii

Chapter 1 Learning the Law, Turning to Politics 1
Two Shoemakers 4
Parallel Lives on Center Street 7
The Deans of the Hampshire County Bar 13
162 King Street 17
63 Center Street 19

Chapter 2 Eight More Years a Bachelor 21
The Cupid at Clarke School 21
Moving North 22
Shared Interests 25
The Introduction 26
Losing Touch 27
Eating at Rahar's Inn 29
George Washington Cable 31
40 Round Hill Road 32

Chapter 3 Newlywed 35
Renting a Library of Classics 36
The Norwood Hotel, 31 Bridge Street 38
5 Crescent Street 39

Chapter 4 The Settled Life	43
The Neighbors Who Were So Kind	43
19-21 Massasoit Street	57
Chapter 5 Best Home for the Coolidges	59
Building The Beeches	59
A Modest Place	64
Conclusion	71
References	75
Notes	79
About the Author	92

Acknowledgments

The homes of Calvin Coolidge in Northampton, Massachusetts yield many untold tales. The thirtieth president's dwellings and the people associated with them—people Coolidge roomed with and the neighbors he encountered—reveal his character and personality.

A few years ago, I heard a panel of four local novelists speak at a Main Street, Northampton bookstore. A member of the audience asked if any of them worked from an outline. All of the authors said the characters guided the development of their stories. Although this is not a work of fiction, one 'character', Robert Weir, steward of Clarke School for the Deaf, inspired me to write this book. When I discovered that he had served on the City Common Council while Coolidge roomed with him, I wondered if Coolidge only associated with people interested in politics. When I discovered that another landlord had been on the Board of Selectmen in the Town of Williamsburg before moving into Northampton, I saw more evidence for my theory. Rob Weir's story became compelling. As I found out more about him, he seemed to be saying that in some accounts of Coolidge, writers only allude to him by job title, and if they use his name, they sometimes get it wrong. It was time to tell the story of this man and his family with whom Coolidge roomed for eight years and of the others who influenced and observed him as he went about securing one of life's basic needs—housing.

As time wore on, the decidedly nasal voice of Calvin himself gave me advice:

> Nothing in the world can take the place of Persistence. Talent will not; nothing is more common than unsuccessful men with talent. Genius will not; unrewarded genius is almost a proverb. Education will not; the world is full of educated derelicts. Persistence and Determination alone are omnipotent. The slogan "Press On," has solved and always will solve the problems of the human race.
>
> (Calvin Coolidge, 1932)

In the here and now, Julie Bartlett, archivist at the Calvin Coolidge Presidential Library and Museum, decided to assign me, her new volunteer with a background in local real estate, to the housing research files of Joseph Harrison, former librarian and Coolidge Collection founder. I will never be able to thank her enough. It takes many people to produce even a small volume like this, and I have no doubt forgotten someone, an oversight for which I apologize in advance. I do owe a huge debt to people who helped with the research, including Nanci Young and the Smith College Archives staff; the town clerk of Williamsburg, Massachusetts; the city clerk of Northampton and her staff; and Alan Marvelli, Jim Cooke, George Snook, Daisy Mathias and Bob Nelson, Rita Bleiman, Susan Williams, and Lu Stone. Helen Wise was a wonderful editor; J. R. Greene, Anne Arsenault, Catherine Wright, and MJ Jecklin read what I had hoped might be the last draft. Thanks to all of you.

Photo Credits

All photos are courtesy of the Calvin Coolidge Memorial Library and Museum, except those on pages 17, 19, and 33 that were taken by the author. The Grant family photograph on page 47 was used with assistance from the Rockefeller Archives.

Chronology of Calvin Coolidge's Life and Homes in Northampton, Massachusetts

1872   July 4—Born in Plymouth Notch, Vermont

1879   January 3—Grace Anna Goodhue born in Burlington, Vermont

1891   Enters Amherst College, Amherst, Massachusetts

1895   June—Graduates from Amherst College
September—Settles in Northampton, Massachusetts to study the law and rents a room at **162 King Street**

1896   Rents a room at **63 Center Street** in the same house as Robert B. Weir

1897   Robert B. Weir appointed steward of Clarke School for the Deaf; Coolidge rooms with Weir at **40 Round Hill Road**

1905   October 4—Coolidge marries Grace Anna Goodhue, a teacher at Clarke School; after a Montreal honeymoon, they reside at the **Norwood Hotel** while looking for a suitable rental
November—The Coolidges move to **5 Crescent Street**, home of a professor on sick leave from Smith College

1906   August—They move to **21 Massasoit Street**, half a duplex house that will be their home for 24 years

      September 7—Birth of first son, John Calvin

1907-1908   Coolidge serves two terms as state representative

1908   April 13—Birth of second son, Calvin, Jr.

1910-1911   Serves as mayor of Northampton for two one-year terms

1912-1915   Serves as state senator; 1914-1915 as state senate president

1916-1918   Serves as lieutenant governor

1919   Serves as governor for two years; Boston police strike in 1919 brings Coolidge national attention

1920 Elected vice president of the United States; term begins March 1921

1923 August 3—Becomes president of the United States upon the death of Warren G. Harding

1924 July 7—Death of Calvin Coolidge, Jr. in Washington, D.C. from blood poisoning

November 4—Elected president of the United States

1929 March—Returns to Northampton to live on Massasoit Street as a private citizen

1930 April—the Coolidges buy their first real estate in Massachusetts, The Beeches, **16 Hampton Terrace** but wait to move until mid-May

1933 January 5—Calvin Coolidge dies at The Beeches

1957 July 8—Grace Coolidge dies in Northampton

Preface

Calvin Coolidge lived in Northampton, Massachusetts for thirty-seven years except for his eight-year sojourn in the nation's capital. He was a brand new graduate of Amherst College when he arrived in September 1895 to study the law and was the former president of the United States when he died in January 1933. During his first years in the city, he lived the life of a quiet country lawyer with a gift, some said genius, for politics. However, after he served as mayor of Northampton in 1910 and 1911, his life took an extraordinary turn. He went places that few dared imagine while his fellow citizens watched his progress.

Time spent making the transition from college student to independent adult are critical for most people. From the beginning, the law community and the political life of this small New England city shaped the future president.

However, the practical issues presented by day-to-day living were also influencing him in noticeable ways. Until he married Grace Goodhue in 1905, Coolidge rented single rooms, and then after a short time in a local hotel, the couple rented a furnished home for nine months. For the next twenty-four years, they lived in half of a rented duplex house that they made world-famous. After the White House, the Coolidges purchased the best house for their needs, which arguably was and is the best house in town.

The landlords and the neighbors influenced the man, and he made an impression on them as well. Some spoke about him as he became prominent in local, state, and national politics. Most stressed that he was shy and reserved, but others did not stop there. They recognized that he would be successful, but few, if any, predicted that he would hold all the offices he did—city councilor, state representative, mayor, state senator, president of the state senate, lieutenant governor, governor of Massachusetts, vice president and president of the United States.

Calvin Coolidge is the only U.S. president born on the Fourth of July. This unique event took place in 1872 in tiny Plymouth Notch, Vermont in the living quarters behind his father's general store. The hamlet consisted of the store, a church, a school, and a cemetery scattered among about a half dozen houses, mostly inhabited by Coolidge's kinfolk, including four devoted grandparents. His own small family included his parents, John Calvin Coolidge and Victoria Josephine Moor Coolidge, and his younger sister, Abigail, born in 1875. When Calvin was a boy, his mother was never in the best of health. She died at age

This studio portrait of Coolidge with bowler hat and cane was taken during his days at Amherst College, 1891-1895.

thirty-nine when he was twelve years old. Since there was no high school in little Plymouth, after completing his studies in the local one-room school, he went on to the Black River Academy in Ludlow, Vermont, twelve miles from home. When he was eighteen years old, his lively, red-headed sister, Abbie, died at the age of fifteen. Calvin was to leave Vermont the following fall for college in Amherst, Massachusetts, where he would become a member of the Amherst College Class of 1895 and would later serve as a college trustee.

However, this book is not a biography of Calvin Coolidge. Instead it shows how a young professional, living on his own, made his way in the world more than one hundred years ago. Focusing on the homes themselves and the people associated with these seven Northampton residences, it paints a picture of Coolidge from a very intimate perspective. The neighbors and landlords have interesting personal stories of their own that contribute to the rich detail available about the president's Northampton, giving a feel for life here during the early years of the last century. The book also tries to answer questions such as: how did he decide where to live, who were his roommates or housemates, and what did they think of him?

Public figures usually have private lives, at least before they became famous. Coolidge interacted with all types of people, often winning their respect and sometimes the vote of a good number that a modern political analyst might not identify as "Coolidge voters." Both Grace and Calvin had friendships with neighbors, exchanging advice about gardening and childrearing. Calvin attended the events and did the things that citizens expect of their mayor, state representative or state senator. He was a regular at the Edwards Church Men's Club, although only Grace was a church member. He mentored a committeewoman in the state Republican Party while Grace organized voter registration drives for women and was very involved with the church, Clarke School for the Deaf, and her sons' schools.

Coolidge's early housing followed the pattern of many young, single people of any era. In his first ten years in Northampton before marrying, Coolidge rented a series of rooms at 162 King Street, 63 Center Street, and 40 Round Hill Road. In the 1890s, it was unusual for a single person to rent an apartment. Normally, young people living away from their families rented people's spare rooms, and that was what the future president did. Coolidge had experienced similar arrangements during his high school and college years and should have been an old hand at 'rooming'.

When the Coolidges married, they lived in the Norwood Hotel for a short time before finding a furnished home to rent from a Smith College professor at 5 Crescent Street. The new bride had planned to do her own housework, but this home came with a housekeeper so she was spared the duties.

Today, the Coolidges are associated primarily with the last two houses they occupied. They lived a settled life in a duplex or half house at 21 Massasoit Street from August 1906 to May 1930, first as a family and later as a couple. Like most politicians, Coolidge remained registered to vote in his home district and so this house was his official residence. The first couple continued to pay rent, and various family members lived there through most of Calvin's presidency. Few state or national office holders have rented their primary residences and shared it with another family, now or then, so these circumstances are unusual in American history. In 1930, the Coolidges bought a home—the first real estate they owned in Massachusetts. The Beeches, the large estate where the former president spent his last years, was a retreat from the world, physically satisfying—private with large grounds for his dogs, room to entertain out-of-town guests, and within walking distance to downtown—but possibly isolating for his gregarious wife. However, at that time their celebrity status afforded the Coolidges limited housing choices.

On April 10, 1940, the local newspaper, the *Daily Hampshire Gazette*, published this short item that was the impetus for the first surviving research about Coolidge's homes:

> A recent book on the life of Calvin Coolidge places his early days in Northampton as on Center [S]treet, while the city directory of 1896 and 1897 says he roomed at 162 King [S]treet with Mr. and Mrs. Charles Lavake. This later fact is substantiated by the couple's granddaughter, Mrs. William Marsh, 27[3] Crescent [S]treet, who remembers seeing Coolidge there when visiting her grandparents. The Northampton directory of 1898 places Mr. Coolidge on Round Hill. Does anyone know of Calvin Coolidge's living in other places during his early years in Northampton?   – C.H.L.

The 1940 book the *Gazette* writer referred to is *Calvin Coolidge: The Man From Vermont* by Claude M. Fuess. On page 80, the author wrote, "When Coolidge first arrived in Northampton he lived, according to a well-authenticated report, in the Lyman House at 63 Center Street, in an upstairs room."

The *Gazette* item sparked a burst of activity by local historians during the next two months. Clifford H. Lyman, who owned a prominent bookstore, was the "C.H.L." who wrote the newspaper item. (It was not his house that Fuess referred to as "the Lyman house" but the home of a distant cousin.) Joseph L. Harrison, librarian of Forbes, Northampton's public library, was in contact with him and Charles Dean, a writer and poet. Harrison created a four-page, double-spaced manuscript with the information given by the people who contacted the trio and reported the results of a search of the city directories between 1896-97 and 1933. (Coolidge was listed in the city directory dated 1895-96, but that very helpful entry was not mentioned.) It appears that many people were in touch with these men, and it was while fact-checking Harrison's work (hereafter referred to as the Harrison manuscript) that the idea for this book arose.

Today people often ask where Coolidge lived, hoping, with good reason, that seeing the former president's houses will give them insights into his personality and preferences. Coolidge usually associated with genial people interested in politics and public life, and he always lived within a short walk or trolley ride to his office—at 59 Main Street while a student and at 25 Main Street while a lawyer and political figure. When he rented rooms, the first and second were modest, befitting a thrifty law student, and the third was in a more substantial building appropriate for a new lawyer and with a good Ward 2 address helpful for a budding Republican politician. After he married, his first long-term residence was comfortable and economical—a far cry from the spacious, secluded home where he spent his last few years.

Chapter 1
Learning the Law, Turning to Politics

Rhoda Lavake told her granddaughter that the new occupant of her spare room was genial and neat but not talkative. In the fall of 1895, she was one of the first people in the city, but far from the last, to express this opinion about the new law student at the office of Hammond and Field, Calvin Coolidge.

In his first two years in Northampton, Coolidge lived a law student's life—lots of study and very little leisure—while renting a room in two different houses, first with the Lavakes and then with the John Lyman family. After his first week in town, he wrote to his father that he was getting along all right, but would not have time to read the Vermont newspaper that his father had offered to send to him. But even during this intensely focused period of his life, he found time for his first modest forays into practical politics and for some recreation.

Coolidge related that, after earning his bachelor's degree, "I went home to do a summer's work on the farm, which was to be my last. I had decided to enter the law and expected to attend a law school, but one of my classmates wrote me late in the summer that there was an opportunity to go into the office of Hammond and Field at Northampton." The friend who let him know about this opening and thereby changed U.S. history was Ernest W. Hardy, a Northampton native who was studying with another local lawyer.

The young Coolidge debated his future with his father during his junior and senior year at Amherst. Calvin may have favored the "law school" alternative strongly because he told his father that he would be living his adulthood in the new century, and it would be futile to prepare himself by the methods of the past.

"Reading" the law was, however, an acceptable way to prepare for a locally administered oral bar exam at the turn of the last century. It was like apprenticing. Coolidge graduated from Amherst College in June 1895 and began his law studies at 59 Main Street, Northampton in late September. Late in his life, he noted that it was one thing to know how to pass the bar exam and another to know how to practice the law. He believed his education in a law office had advantages because while he read the law books, he also observed in court and drew up simple documents from the beginning of his studies. Already in his first year, he invested some of the thirty dollars per month that his father sent to cover living expenses in law textbooks that provided interpretation of the main legal principles he would need to know.

When Coolidge was accepted into their law office, John C. Hammond and Henry P. Field, graduates of Amherst College in 1865 and 1880 respectively, were prominent attorneys. During Coolidge's first months there, Field was elected mayor of the city, and Hammond was elected district attorney. Although the partners already had one law student, Edward Shaw, a second scholar certainly would have been welcomed with the two principals in the firm otherwise occupied. Each partner had long lists of civic accomplishments and according to a 1902 account, the firm "has been on one side or the other of most of the important cases in this county" since its formation. Although that sounds like hyperbole, Coolidge confirmed that Hammond was "considered the leader of the Hampshire Bar," and the *Daily Hampshire Gazette* called both men the "dean of the local bar" in their respective obituaries.

This law office was certainly the best place in the city for an ambitious young politician to begin. In perhaps his first political foray, Coolidge helped in Henry Field's mayoral campaign by handing out literature at a meeting in Ward 6. In a second political act also suggested by Field, Coolidge wrote a letter to the editor of the *Gazette* in defense of the gold standard. It appeared on August 6, 1896 in the middle of the Bryan/McKinley presidential election campaign. Coolidge's choice, the Ohio Republican William McKinley, was elected and carried Northampton.

All through his childhood, when he attended town meeting or observed in his family's parlor, Coolidge saw adults with common sense and character taking leadership roles in their community. His chief role model was his father, who served three two-year terms as a Vermont state representative beginning in 1872, the year Calvin was born. The elder Coolidge knew Vermont's leaders including the governors, senators, and the congressman and would acquire the title "Colonel" when he served on the governor's staff as an aide-de-camp in 1900. It was perhaps the colonel's long list of local offices, including selectman, school superintendent, and tax collector that inspired his son during the law student years. According to Fuess, "Colonel Coolidge was an inveterate politician, whose shrewdness and discretion was transmitted to his son."

Before his move to Northampton, the younger Coolidge's correspondence with his father showed his budding interest in politics. When his college friend John Percival (Percy) Deering of Saco, Maine arrived in Amherst for their senior year, Calvin told his father about Republican results in a recent Maine election.

Besides his father and mentors at his law office, Coolidge's fellow young attorneys were setting good examples of community service. Many had also trained with Hammond and Field.

Coolidge did take some breaks from his studies. Not known later in life as a 'joiner', Coolidge reported spending some Sunday afternoons at a canoe club on the Connecticut River, known as the Wish-Ton-Wish Club.

Coolidge had made the transition from student to lawyer by the time this portrait was taken in 1905.

Only twenty-one months after beginning his studies, Coolidge took the bar exam and was admitted to the bar on July 2, 1897, the nicest of early birthday presents.

Two Shoemakers

While still a student at Amherst College, Coolidge went to a Northampton shoemaker's shop at 18 Gothic Street and met its proprietor, James Lucey. Three students walked into Lucey's shop that day to have their shoes repaired. Since Coolidge needed his fixed while he waited, the other two men occupied their time by debating a point from one of their recent classes. One of them asked Coolidge what he thought, and Lucey later recalled that after some hesitation, Coolidge said that they were both wrong. The shoemaker was very impressed with the young man's further explanation and invited him back to talk some more. On that day a relationship between the tradesman and the future president began, resulting in a friendship treasured by both. Coolidge often returned for informal political discussions at Lucey's shop, which became a meeting place for a group of Irish Democrats who supported Coolidge because they had come to know him there. Phil Gleason, the blacksmith; Ed Lynch, the mason; and Johnny Dewey, the tavern keeper, converted other Democrats to Coolidge, the Republican political candidate.

The first floor shop on Gothic Street, where Lucey typically spent fourteen hours each day, was a few steps down from sidewalk level. His family lived above: his wife, two sons, and six daughters.

When Coolidge suddenly became president in 1923 after Warren G. Harding's death, he wrote a note to his old friend, Jim Lucey, dated August 6, three days after he was sworn in, that immediately became famous:

> My Dear Mr. Lucey
>
> Not often do I see you or write to you, but I want you to know that if it were not for you I should not be here, and I want to tell you how much I love you.
>
> Do not work too much and try to enjoy yourself in your well earned leisure of age.
>
>   Yours Sincerely,
>   Calvin Coolidge

The Lucey note was often reprinted or quoted in the media because people were eager for information about the new chief executive. Vice presidents were no better known at that time than they are today. Soon the shoemaker/philosopher was famous nationwide, because many reporters came to Northampton to interview this surprisingly important person in the new president's life, who also had the gift to be quotable. They flocked to the shop to find the letter framed and hanging on the wall. This friendship lasted until Coolidge's death, when Lucey told a reporter that he had lost the best friend he ever had.

Jim Lucey reveled in Coolidge becoming president. He told a reporter who sought him out, "I realized that here was a most unusual young man. I had never met one exactly like him. No, I never had any ideas about his becoming President, but I predicted that he would go far." The shoemaker called Coolidge shy and reserved and noted that he was silent if the mood struck him or talkative if a topic stirred his interest. "You might mistake his restraint for indifference though I never knew a man who was more interested in a wider variety of things and people....He is not cold and distant, but he is modest and self-contained. The man thinks; he doesn't talk."

Much was made of the president's use of the word 'love' in the note. Sheet music for a song titled, "The President's Love Letter," exists. However, it was not the only time that the president used the four-letter word in written communication not sent to his wife or family. When his mentor, John C. Hammond, died the *Gazette* published a letter from Coolidge to Hammond's son, Thomas, which contained the phrase "The one we love has gone."

It is possible that Mr. Lucey was instrumental in Coolidge finding his first room to rent in the home of another shoemaker, Charles Lavake. Beginning in the fall of 1895, Coolidge lodged with Charles Lavake and his wife, Rhoda, at 162 King Street. By Mrs. Lavake's criteria, he was a good tenant. The Lavakes, a couple in their seventies, had had roomers in their home as early as 1860, according to the U.S. Census. Rhoda Williams Lavake was born in Williamsburg just a few miles from her final home. Her Northampton-born husband, Charles Lavake, had an unusual last name but he was not a new immigrant or even the son of an immigrant. His father, William, had been a shoemaker as well, and various members of the family had lived on King Street for generations. It was just before the American Revolution that the first will for someone with the same last name was probated in Hampshire County.

The Lavake house was not in a highly desirable location so how did Coolidge happen to rent a room there? The Boston and Maine Railroad yard was across the street, and although less busy than it is today, King Street was still the main north/south thoroughfare. The house was also a considerable walk from Coolidge's law office at the corner of Main and King Street. A search of the *Gazette* during the month of September 1895 shows no advertisement for a room in any house, so word-of-mouth must have been the means of advertising in that era. When Coolidge moved to town, he probably knew only five people who could help him find housing: his teachers/mentors, Hammond and Field; the other law student at the office, Edward Shaw; his friend, who told him about the opening, Ernest Hardy; and the man who would become the nation's most famous shoemaker, Jim Lucey.

Some people simply rented rooms from others, and they were called 'roomers'. Others who rented space with some combination of meals, laundry or maid service provided were known as 'boarders'. Coolidge only talked about his housing after he passed the bar and was practicing law, describing himself as a roomer who took his meals out. It is unclear whether he took his meals from the Lavakes.

Widows commonly became landladies for economic reasons, renting spare rooms after the death of their husbands, but Coolidge never rented a room from a woman alone. Each of his very different landlords rented rooms for reasons beyond their basic need for income: an older couple whose children had left home; a middle-aged couple with two children, the father having suffered a business reversal; and a young single man who needed to fill his empty apartment. It is hard to find information about these rentals today because there were probably no leases to leave a paper trail. Even if there had been a lease, the families renting him the first two rooms had no inkling that the quiet law student would become president so they had no reason to save any evidence of their relationship with him. Both of the first two couples had died by June 1905, before Coolidge was married or had become mayor.

The Lavakes' granddaughter, Bertha Marsh, living with her own small family at 273 Crescent Street, remembered seeing Coolidge when she visited. She said that he brought his books into the living room to study with little regard for what the family was doing there at the time. Unfortunately, her opportunities to get to know him were limited because her grandmother died on June 3, 1896 at the age of seventy-four. It is not clear how long Coolidge remained there after that, but he certainly had left before Mr. Lavake died on September 18, 1897.

The Harrison manuscript states that Coolidge roomed and boarded at The Hampton Hotel, 51 Pleasant Street, when William E. Cooney was the proprietor. The establishment opened in the summer of 1896, and the 1896-97 city directory is the only one that shows Cooney as the proprietor. In May 1897, the *Gazette* reported that F. A. Reed was to be the new manager. Coolidge most likely stayed at the Hampton while Mrs. Lavake was ill or immediately after her death before he found a new room at 63 Center Street.

Parallel Lives on Center Street

John W. Lyman and Henry E. Maynard led curiously parallel lives. They bought neighboring homes on Center Street in the same year, 1884. They died within two days of each other in May 1905 before Coolidge, Lyman's former roomer and Maynard's neighbor, became famous. Both men had varied careers, but their last jobs were with the city. Lyman was a clerk for the highway department during his last seven years, and Maynard was chief of police for eight years ending in January 1905. Maybe these parallels were just coincidence and did not lead the two men to become friends. There is no evidence that they were more than neighbors. In fact, their twelve-year age difference alone may argue against a close relationship, but one member of the Maynard family was aware of the tenants next door.

Henry Maynard's daughter, Mabel, reported that Calvin Coolidge had lived next door to her family in the Lyman's house at 63 Center Street. She was a vocal music teacher and soloist who lived and worked at 57 Center Street from July 1884 until her death in December 1948. According to her, Coolidge's room was in the right wing or ell on the second floor near one rented by Robert Weir, who was at that time a clerk at the S. E. Bridgman Bookstore at 108 Main Street and later became Coolidge's third Northampton landlord.

Miss Maynard gave no dates for Coolidge's residing next door, but Mary Lyman, John's wife, died June 1, 1897. If the two men still lived there, Coolidge's studying for the bar would have been disrupted only one month before the exam. On the other hand, the Lymans' single daughter, Carrie, was in her thirties and capable of handling the roomers with only limited interruption, so they were not necessarily sent away to fend for themselves. Lyman, his daughter and a roomer made up the household in the 1900 U.S. Census. Miss Maynard did tell Harrison that the men took their meals out, making it easier to believe that they may have stayed. If they were unable to remain, there would have been a gap of two months before August 1, 1897 when Weir started his work as steward of Clarke School, a position that included housing. Researchers for the Northampton Historical Commission state that Coolidge spent summers in the home of John C. Hammond, 222 Elm Street, while the Hammond family vacationed in nearby Goshen. This summer was one when he might have needed housing.

Mabel Maynard was in her early twenties when the two men lived next door. Her age would have made her a possible romantic interest for either Weir or Coolidge. Ishbel Ross noted in her biography of Grace Coolidge that when the couple met, he was recovering from having a marriage proposal turned down by a red-headed Northampton girl. This unnamed woman remained single and sometimes wondered why she had been "indifferent to Calvin Coolidge."

Coolidge had a personal relationship of some kind with another woman, Rozella (Rose) Deering, a Smith College student from 1899 to 1901. She was the younger sister of his Amherst College friend Percy Deering. However, Rose married in 1903 so she doesn't completely fit the profile. In the 1960s when Ross was writing Grace's biography, someone in Miss Deering's position would more likely be called a college girl or a 'Smithie', not a Northampton girl.

Coolidge and Maynard's fathers were businessmen and public servants so they had something in common. Although not a college graduate like his future wife, Mabel was an accomplished musician singing in the choir of the Unitarian Church around the turn of the last century. Whether or not Mabel was the "red-haired girl," she could have dated one of her neighbors, although there is no evidence that she ever did. However, her age, background, accomplishments, and proximity make for intriguing speculation.

Unfortunately, both Henry Maynard and his daughter, Mabel, suffered from diabetes at the end of their lives. In those days before insulin treatments, he had been so ill at least twice that it was thought that he would die and surgery was necessary.

Born in Enfield, Connecticut in 1848, Maynard was more traveled than Coolidge or his neighbor, John Lyman, because he had gone to St. Louis to join a brother in business. After a year in Missouri, he returned to New England and worked for the Boston Street Railway for two years. He moved to Connecticut to learn the barber's trade before first owning a shop in Easthampton, Massachusetts and later in Northampton beginning in 1873. Maynard joined Northampton's police force in 1882 and was appointed its chief five years later.

The Lyman family came to the city in July 1884 when Mary Lucy Matthews Lyman bought 63 Center Street and lived there with her husband, John Wright Lyman, and two children, Carrie and Quartus. Born in 1836, Mr. Lyman was the son of a successful Easthampton farmer and graduated from Williston Academy in his hometown.

In the Civil War, he served for one year as a corporal with the Fifty-second Massachusetts Regiment and was a partner in Woodard and Lyman, a button manufacturing company in Williamsburg, when he returned. He was active in the business and civic life of the town, and elected master of the Hampshire Lodge of Masons. It was the failure of his business in June 1884 that perhaps caused the family to move into the city and take in roomers. The *Gazette* reported on June 24, 1884 that the factory employing about twenty workers had been closed, and its affairs turned over to Mr. Woodard.

Upon arriving in Northampton, Lyman opened a wholesale fruit and produce company on Main Street. During the time that Coolidge was living with the family, Lyman's daughter, Carrie, was the proprietor of a confectionery/lunch room at 279 Main Street, and her father was its manager. A florist with greenhouses on Prospect Street had a counter within the Lymans' store, and the premises remained a flower shop after the Lymans' business closed.

Both Maynard and Lyman, like most friends and acquaintances of Calvin Coolidge, are described as generous, gregarious people. Maynard was known to have a large heart and an impulsive temperament—quick to anger and equally quick to respond to other people's problems. He was known to use his own money to supplement the police budget when it ran low. His obituary specifically mentioned that he was a natural commander and an avid lover of nature and the outdoors. Similarly, Lyman's obituary described him as a genial man, a good accountant, and a good person to deal with the public. It also noted that Lyman was chairman of the Williamsburg Board of Selectmen—another Coolidge associate with an interest in public service. A search of that town's records from 1878 to 1885 showed that he held a few minor offices such as elector under the provisions of the will of Oliver Smith in the late 1870s. He was elected to the Board of Selectmen and became its chair in the fateful year of 1884, therefore only serving until his business failed and he moved to Northampton in July.

However, the selectmen's race that year was far from ordinary. Lyman was elected with Edwin F. Miller and Henry C. Smith. All three men were new to the board, no one having been re-elected from the previous year. The annual town meeting was scheduled for Monday, March 3, but the *Hampshire Gazette and Northampton Courier*'s reporter began his story on February 26. A large turnout was expected because the entire Board of Selectmen was being opposed. Its members had managed to anger two factions during the past year. On one side were the "liquor" men or license party and on the other, the temperance party, better known in history books as "the wets and the drys."

The previous town meeting had voted to license drinking establishments, but the town's hotels were within 400 feet of the schools so no licenses could be granted. The result was liquor being sold freely in these establishments without licenses, as illegal as that was. The liquor men were talking of running two men for the board, and the temperance side was hoping that strategy would split the "liquor" vote to give them all three seats on the board, which is exactly what happened. The *Gazette and Courier* reported and editorialized:

> The result of voting for officers was quite a surprise to many; the temperance ticket for selectmen being elected entire[ly] by the temperance and law and order men....The temperance party having now obtained complete possession of the town government, with a no license vote to back them up, it remains to be seen how wisely they will administer. They will have the best wishes of all good citizens.

In a lesson about the importance of every vote, the results were very close: Lyman, 161; E. F. Miller, 160; Smith, 145; O'Neil, 144; Carter, 135; Banks, 121; A. P. Miller, 30; others, 2; total vote cast, 320.

Soon the new selectmen decided to license two drugstores to sell liquor for medicinal purposes, and no doubt in an early effort to make local government more transparent, they scheduled their meetings for the town hall every Saturday from 2 to 4 p.m. The temperance victory was short-lived and by the next year's town meeting, Lyman had moved from Williamsburg, Henry Smith had been re-elected to the board and Edwin Miller had not. The two new selectmen were John O'Neil and Thomas Carter, the fourth and fifth place vote getters in the previous year's election.

It is likely that Coolidge absorbed a good deal about temperance politics while living at the Lyman house since he was not always cloistered in his room, and his fellow roomer, Rob Weir, was the grandson of a temperance lecturer and publisher. Hampshire County felt the full force of the temperance debate, and Coolidge was affected by the issue in his campaigns at all levels. The newspaper had a pro-temperance article on the front page of almost every weekly issue that spring. In 1905, there were seven temperance societies listed in the city—three were chapters of the Women's Christian Temperance Union and the other four seemed to have more direct religious connections. For example, Jim Lucey, the shoemaker, belonged to the Father Matthew Temperance Society.

Temperance had been debated since the early nineteenth century and with greater passion after the Civil War. The U.S. Constitution's Eighteenth Amendment and the Volstead Act were passed in 1919 and went into effect in January 1920, a little over a year before Coolidge was inaugurated vice president. Prohibition ended with the Twenty-first Amendment in December 1933 so Coolidge was the president most associated with this social and legal experiment.

The issue reportedly played a part in Coolidge's first race for mayor in 1909. His opponent was Harry Bicknell, a local merchant, who had argued the pro-temperance position in a debate at the Edwards Church where Grace Coolidge was a fellow member. Bicknell took the position just so that there would be someone on both sides. The wets were not amused and demanded an explanation of his position during the campaign. Unfortunately, what he said pleased neither side.

Coolidge characteristically said little, offended no drys and found that his legal services for a brewery and Northampton's bartenders had enhanced his stature among the wets. This strategy paid off with a win by the slim margin of 187 votes. Later, Bicknell became mayor in 1922 and 1923 in time to send Coolidge congratulations when he became president.

The temperance issue arose again in Coolidge's races for lieutenant governor and governor. In May 1920, he vetoed a bill authorizing the sale of 2.75 percent beer in the Commonwealth because at that time it was against the U.S. Constitution, a good move politically when the Prohibition forces were at their greatest strength.

Like the Williamsburg Board of Selectmen and Harry Bicknell, Coolidge later found himself in the middle negotiating his way between the sides. It soon became clear that effective enforcement of Prohibition would be expensive and difficult on many levels. Historians disagree about whether Coolidge was enthusiastic about enforcing the law. The president was known to allow almost everyone in his administration to do their jobs without much interference from him. Coolidge's biographer McCoy wrote, "It was clear that the President was directing the Attorney General and the Secretary of the Treasury to make of Prohibition laws what their own consciences required." Therefore both cabinet members were criticized for lax enforcement. On the other hand, the Coolidges did not serve alcohol in the White House. One biographer believed that Coolidge upheld the Prohibition statutes because they were the law of the land, but noted that the president said, "Any law that inspires disrespect for other laws—the good laws—is a bad law." In this way, the president may have communicated his true feelings.

Colonel Theodore Roosevelt, the son of the former president, had occasion to advise Coolidge, rather tongue-in-cheek, to tell Congress that a billion dollars would be needed to successfully enforce the law. Roosevelt hoped that naming what at the time was a huge amount of money would start a discussion that would bring an end to Prohibition.

Luckily, both men knew a good joke when they heard one. Roosevelt's advice caused Coolidge to make one of his more quotable remarks: "Colonel, never go out to meet trouble. If you will just sit still, nine times out of ten, [someone] will intercept it before it reaches you."

The Deans of the Hampshire County Bar

Today law students spend a lot of time in law libraries. For Coolidge, studying the law meant being in the Hammond and Field office at 59 Main Street for long hours. It was his home away from home. He probably spent as much time there as he spent at 162 King or 63 Center Street. The building was on the northeast corner of King and Main Streets, and the offices were on the second floor above a bank. The structure Coolidge knew was demolished to make way for the Art Deco building that opened on this site in the fall of 1928 and still occupies that corner today.

John C. Hammond practiced law with various partners in this location for fifty-six years before he died on April 21, 1926. From 1888 to 1903, his partner was Henry P. Field. Their partnership lasted until Hammond's son, Thomas, became an attorney. Field recalled at the time of Hammond's death that in their fifteen years together, they had had no partnership agreement and no disagreements.

Coolidge described and thanked both men in his autobiography: "The senior member of the law firm was John C. Hammond, who was considered the leader of the Hampshire Bar. He was a lawyer of great learning and wide business experience...He was massive and strong rather than elegant, and placed great stress on accuracy. The junior member was Henry P. Field, an able lawyer and a man of engaging personality and polish, who I found was an alderman. That appeared to me at the time to be close to the Almighty in importance. I shall always remember with a great deal of gratitude the kindness of these two men to me." One of Field's cherished possessions was a copy of Coolidge's autobiography inscribed, "To Henry P. Field who helped make this book possible. With regards, Calvin Coolidge."

Hammond commented on Coolidge saying, "I had never seen such a man, especially a young man. I couldn't understand how a man could be so quiet and seem to care for nothing outside of his work." Hammond seems later to have developed a more favorable impression of Coolidge because Calvin reported to his father in the summer of 1897 that this mentor would be happy to have Coolidge settle in Northampton and practice law there. Judge Field was never known to suggest that he had anything to do with Coolidge's success. However, Field's mentoring of Coolidge continued until a deep friendship developed. In 1906,

Coolidge was elected to his first term as state representative, which coincided with Field's most influential period with the state Republican Party. Field accompanied his friend to Boston on the first day of the session and introduced him to the party's leadership. At least two of their number were reported later to have been unimpressed. Coolidge also had in his pocket a letter of introduction to the speaker of the house from Northampton attorney Richard Irwin, who had been a state representative, "This will introduce you to the new member-elect from my town, Calvin Coolidge. Like a singed cat, he is better than he looks."

When Coolidge died in 1933, Field wrote as a close friend: "We all knew his fine character, his kindness and consideration for others, his exceptional abilities, his genius for government, his strong common sense, his keen sense of humor…And we also knew how unpretentious he was…And yet this quiet friend and fellow citizen of ours retired from the presidency the most highly esteemed and most popular man in all these United States."

At the time of Field's death, a *Gazette* editorial writer claimed that no man was more of an "intimate" of Coolidge than the judge but that Field "indicated that one usually 'knew' Calvin Coolidge just so much—and no more." If this is an accurate assessment, it is very significant because the judge was indeed a Coolidge intimate.

Both Hammond and Field were leaders of the bar and the community as well. After his term as district attorney, Hammond was president of the Massachusetts Bar Association in 1913 and was called 'judge' although he had no judicial appointment. Field was president of the local bar association from 1919 until his death in 1937. He had been either a special judge or the permanent judge of the probate court since 1909.

Hammond served on the board of Clarke School for the Deaf, the Home Culture Clubs, Williston Academy, Hopkins Academy, Massachusetts Hospital for Consumptive and Tubercular Patients in Rutland, and the Metropolitan Park Commission. He took great interest in Northampton's civic projects, spending twenty years on the sewer commission and establishing the trolley system as director of the Northampton Street Railway Company. The last two involvements were complementary to his avocation, real estate development. He and John A. Sullivan purchased and sold lots on the present streets of Harrison Avenue, Dryad's Green, and Forbes Avenue.

Field's community service was no less impressive. He was mayor of the city for one year in 1896 and again in 1898. He was a Republican State Committeeman who served on the state party executive committee and was a delegate to the national conventions of 1900 and 1904. He was a trustee of the Northampton State Hospital and later served on the Massachusetts State Board of Insanity. During the last fifteen years of his life, Field was a trustee of the Forbes Library and president of its board from 1923 onward. At his death, he bequeathed $30,000 to Forbes, not for buying books but for maintenance of the building. Field's obituary claimed that he had the largest book collection in this part of the state. The judge was a fan of light detective novels as well as the legal tomes and classics that might be expected.

Coolidge was the most successful of the Hammond and Field alumni, but the others also strove to meet the high standards set for them. These men were the future president's contemporaries in his first years of law practice and politics. Edward L. Shaw, the second student in the office with Coolidge, was admitted to the bar on March 3, 1897 and became a Hampshire County judge. Ernest Hardy, who told Coolidge of the opening at Hammond and Field, studied with Attorney Richard W. Irwin and became his law partner. In 1907, he moved to Fargo, North Dakota for a short time and then went on to Portland, Oregon. Before he left Northampton, seventy-five men gathered at the Draper Hotel on Main Street for a farewell banquet at which State Representative Calvin Coolidge served as toastmaster. It would have been interesting had Coolidge spoken formally at this event since the speakers' remarks were printed in full in the *Gazette*. (In 1897, he had told his father that Hardy was the one young lawyer in town who had the same educational advantages he had had and could understand a question of law as well as he could.) Coolidge had dinner at Hardy's home when he visited Portland in 1922 as vice president. Coolidge and Hardy were admitted to the bar on the same day, July 2, 1897.

A third man became a lawyer that day. He was Louis Warner, who had also studied with Hammond and Field and graduated from the Boston Law School. Until moving to Washington, D.C., he practiced with Walter Stevens, another Hammond and Field alumnus, who was admitted to the bar in October 1900. Warner was elected to Northampton's Common Council in 1897 and 1898 and to the Board of Aldermen the next year. From 1900 to 1902, he was elected to three terms as state representative. He served on the Republican city committee and the Common Council. Warner held some of the same offices as Coolidge a few years before the president, maybe setting an example for him. Warner's partner, Stevens, was among the honorary bearers at Coolidge's funeral. Rufus H. Cook passed the bar in 1902 after three years studying at Hammond and Field. He followed Field as a special judge of the probate court in 1923.

When each one of these men gathered at the farewell for Ernest Hardy on a Friday night in 1907, their importance as accomplished country lawyers was reflected in the menu. Clearly, the lavish meals common at this time in big cities were not unheard of in Northampton. The *Gazette* reported the menu as:

> Oysters on Half Shell
> Cream of Lettuce [Soup] with Croutons
> Escalloped Finnan Haddie in Cases
> Olives   Hot-House Cucumbers
> Larded Filet of Beef   Mushroom Sauce
> Browned Potatoes
> Hot-House Tomatoes en Mayonnaise
> Hardy Punch
> Braised Squab   Cider Jelly
> Frozen Ices   Macaroons
> Toasted Crackers and Cheese
> Coffee   Cigarettes   Cigars

The Hammond and Field alumni were considered young men on the rise at the turn of the last century and by 1910, they had 'arrived'. Calvin's election as mayor in the fall of 1909 and again in 1910 punctuated this era.

Coolidge had these words of praise for the local bar in his autobiography: "The ethics of the Northampton Bar were high. It was made up of men who had, and were entitled to have, the confidence and respect of their neighbors who knew them best. They put the interests of their clients above their own, and the public interests above them both. They were courteous and tolerant toward each other and respectful to the court."

162 King Street

This present-day photograph of 12-16 Carpenter Avenue shows Coolidge's first home in Northampton, which was moved to this lot from 162 King Street after September 1906.

Charles Lavake owned the property at 162 King Street from 1872 until his death twenty-five years later. In 1899, his heirs sold it to John J. Moriarty, a builder. Today there is a parking lot on the land that would have been 162 King Street, but in 1940, Joseph Harrison, the Forbes librarian, said that the house was saved and moved to 12-16 Spring Street Avenue (now Carpenter Avenue). Harrison's research revealed that Moriarty moved the house behind its original location and built two houses and a brick commercial block on the original site. That would have happened after September 15, 1906 when Northampton Cooperative Bank sold the Carpenter Avenue lot to Bridget Moriarty, John's wife. The middle building constructed by Moriarty on King

Street was taken down to accommodate today's parking lot and a one-story addition to the brick building on the corner of King and Finn Streets.

The home still standing at 12, 14, and 16 Carpenter Avenue had three attached townhouse-style units at least as early as 1940 when Harrison had contact with Bertha Marsh, the Lavakes' granddaughter. She said that Coolidge lived in the front bedroom over the living room at number 16. According to the present owner, the building might have been a two-family until a rear addition was added to the main 28- by 37-foot structure.

63 Center Street

The striking features of 63 Center Street—its wraparound porch and third-floor dormer—may not have been there in Coolidge's day.

The main part of the side-hall colonial house at 63 Center Street is two-and-a-half stories with a newer shed dormer on the east side of the roof and the gable end facing the street. There is a two-story ell on the east or right side. Today the structure has vinyl clapboard siding and composition roof shingles.

One notable feature of the exterior is the many-angled covered front porch. From the west, the porch extends the full width of the main section of the house and then makes a ninety-degree turn at the east end and runs north along the side of the house perpendicular to the street until it meets the ell. The porch then turns ninety degrees again and extends easterly the width of the house wing.

Mary Lyman, John W. Lyman's wife, purchased 63 Center Street in 1884. Mrs. Lyman's daughter, Carrie, sold the property to Michael and Annie McNamara in 1910. The next generation of the McNamara family may have converted the home to a two-family since in 1940 Mary McNamara, the mayor's secretary, lived in the house and so did her sister and brother-in-law, Frank and Agnes McNamara Shea. Their extended family owned it until 1952. Today it is a multi-family home next to a parking lot for a pharmacy and a neighborhood grocery that faces State Street on an established walking route between Smith College and downtown.

Chapter 2
Eight More Years a Bachelor

For eight years, from 1897 to 1905, Calvin Coolidge lived with the steward of Clarke School for the Deaf, Robert B. Weir, his old housemate at 63 Center Street, and ate his meals at Rahar's Inn. During this time, Coolidge started on three political paths to the nation's highest office—appointed, elected, and party positions. His law career, his move to the house at Clarke School, and his appointment to a political party post began almost simultaneously in 1897, when he became a member of the Republican City Committee for Ward 2. By 1904, he was chair of the committee.

His elected offices began in the late 1890s as well. He joined the City Council in January 1899, where he discovered that the city solicitor position might become open so in anticipation he did not run for re-election. His instincts were correct, and he was appointed city solicitor for the next two years by the city council.

However, Coolidge suffered his first minor setback in January 1902 when Theobald M. Connor, a Democrat who had graduated from Yale and its law school, was given the city solicitor's job by the council instead of him. Perhaps Connor's success was due to his party affiliation, his somewhat superior education or, as Coolidge's biographer Fuess suggests, a firmly established principle of rotation. In 1903 when the Hampshire County Clerk of Courts died, Coolidge was appointed to fill the vacancy. He decided not to run for the full-term elected position because he felt it was a dead end job with little chance for advancement.

The Cupid at Clarke School

Contrary to easy assumptions, Weir's home at 40 Round Hill Road was neither bachelor quarters nor the home of a family with young children. Calvin's tenure at this address embedded him in an adult family with pro-temperance background and leanings. The location was ideal and the nature of the household an interesting change for Coolidge.

Robert B. Weir was the steward of Clarke School for sixteen years. Although the school has no steward today, when Weir married, his occupation was listed as "purchasing agent," perhaps the most accurate definition. The position came with housing, the right half of a brick duplex where the two men lived together, making Weir the person who lived with Coolidge longer than anyone other than his wife and family.

Weir was born in Canada, raised in Tennessee, and joined an aunt to work in Northampton, where he later married. He died in California. While all of these stories are no doubt fascinating, especially if told by Weir—a man credited with great wit, his place as a local legend was secured when he acted as cupid for the future first couple. One day when Coolidge spotted Grace Goodhue out of Weir's window, he asked his landlord to introduce him to her. The introduction and their subsequent marriage were successful by almost every account.

On January 10, 1873, Weir was born in Prescott, Ontario, across the St. Lawrence River from Ogdensburg, New York. He was the first child of his father, Robert, who was born in Scotland, and his mother Jane (Jennie) Moffat, born in Canada. His birth certificate gives his full name as Randolph Balfour Robert Weir, which helps explain why he appears in Northampton records as Randolph B. Weir, Randolph R. B. Weir or Robert B. Weir.

The Weir family moved to Tennessee around 1875. Each of his seven younger siblings was born there. The family lived near his maternal grandparents, John and Lydia Moffat. Grandfather Moffat had been born in 1828 in Glasgow, Scotland. When he was a child, his family moved to Canada where his father abandoned them a few years after their arrival. The younger man struggled to become a teacher. In 1858, he began touring the United States as a temperance lecturer and also editing a temperance magazine. Later, his health deteriorated so he temporarily retired from the lecture circuit in 1869.

Moving North

By the next spring, Moffat had found what he considered a healthy environment at the highest and narrowest place on the Cumberland Plateau between Nashville and Chattanooga, Tennessee. The family settled there and began establishing a summer retreat referred to as a 'Chautauqua of the South' and first called Moffat Station but later known as Monteagle. After the Moffats' era, the retreat eventually became the Highlander Folk School, a training ground for civil rights leaders including Rosa Parks, who attended workshops there before the bus boycott in Montgomery, Alabama.

Rob Weir's aunt, Adelene Moffat, was the first family member to move to Northampton. She came to work for author and social reformer George W. Cable. Eventually, almost all of the Moffat family moved to Massachusetts.

Book tours for authors are not a recent innovation. In June 1887, Cable was on a tour that took him to Nashville. Later that summer, he spent some time at Monteagle, getting to know all generations of the Moffat family. Although grandfather John Moffat had died in 1886, his wife and family provided some stories about him that Cable used in his 1894 novel *John March, Southerner*. Probably John Moffat was a model for John March's father. The sanctimonious Mrs. March is based on either Moffat's wife, Lydia, or their daughter, Jennie Weir. The book's heroine attended a school in the north based on Smith College.

Rob's Aunt Adelene, who was twenty-five years old, was impressed by Cable's ideas for social change and came to Northampton to be his secretary and work for his Home Culture Clubs. Cable had settled in the city a couple of years earlier at the urging of bookstore owner Sidney E. Bridgman, his host during another of his book tours. Miss Moffat came to Northampton in the summer of 1888 and that fall went to New York City to pursue her dream of being an artist. She came back to Northampton the following summer, and although she maintained a studio and gave lessons, gradually she was drawn away from her artistic goals and into the social service and secretarial work of the clubs.

Cable, who founded the Home Culture Clubs in 1887, often said, "The private home is the public hope." Concluding that the most detrimental aspect of society was class distinctions, he set up the clubs to give working people opportunities for learning and discussion in the evenings.

The first club was formed by two Northampton women factory workers, who started a book group. Cable envisioned clubs made up of family members and a few neighbors meeting once a week to read and talk. By 1896, there were about fifty clubs in Northampton and neighboring Easthampton. About twenty more clubs were scattered from

Maine to California. Their number grew to ninety-one clubs in 1898.

The clubs remained home-based until Cable acquired the former Methodist Episcopal Church on Center Street as headquarters in 1892. This building later became the Elks Club and now houses business and residential condos, most notably the Friends Meeting House and the Interfaith Homeless Shelter. Because men and boys seemed to loiter on street corners, a public reading room was opened with them in mind. Casual reading gave way to formal evening classes. Later, there was a great emphasis on horticulture and home gardens.

Like many Northampton organizations before and since, the Home Culture Clubs used Smith College students as volunteers and interns. In 1902, Moffat herself reported that the clubs enjoyed the free services of one hundred young women, most of whom were Smith students. They tutored about three hundred men and women that year. By 1909, the clubs had 227 volunteer teachers from Smith. One who was about to begin teaching penmanship wrote to her mother, "I'm sure I shall be frightened to death when I start to speak to a class—fancy my giving directions to a class of great big working men....But they say that the people who go to learn are very earnest and conscientious."

This student was Gertrude Weil, who wrote a good firsthand description of Weir's Aunt Adelene Moffat and the clubs in another letter home:

> I've never seen people so eager to learn, as they are here. Lots of them come four & five times a week for different things. Servants with only certain nights 'off' go down there to take Elocution, or dancing, or French....I'll speak to Miss Moffat about H. C. Clubs in general....she is the busiest woman I ever saw. She was speaking the other night to some women of a club about to be formed....and she said she had one hour free—on Sunday afternoon—and it would probably be scheduled for that time. And yet when you talk with her, she is just as easy & takes as much interest in each...as if that were the only thing on her mind.

After his father died, Rob Weir came to Northampton to join his aunt and make his way in the world. He was first employed at S. E. Bridgman, Booksellers at 108 Main Street. The first city directory in which he is listed is the 1890-91 edition, as Randolph R. B. Weir, clerk at 108 Main.

His father's death left the family in a poor financial situation, so his mother and five siblings also came to Northampton. His brother, J. Harvey Weir, worked at Bridgman's Bookstore for a short time, but had moved to Springfield by late 1896. Later his youngest brother, Justin, joined the bookshop's staff. Both brothers were associated with the stationery business in California by the 1920s.

Just before Weir started his Clarke School job, he spent the month of July 1897 in Tennessee making arrangements for his mother and siblings to come to live in Northampton in the fall. By 1900, the Weir household at 40 Round Hill Road was Rob Weir; his mother, Jennie; sisters, Mary, Jean and Lydia; brother, Justin; and Calvin Coolidge.

Shared Interests

Coolidge and Weir shared interests as well as housing. Books and politics were two of the most obvious. Coolidge was a voracious reader so it is likely that he and Rob Weir met at the bookstore. Their childhood years in rural settings made both of them yearn from time to time for agricultural pursuits. Coolidge's biographer Fuess wrote that it was also noticed that Calvin got "along well with tradesmen, with clerks in the stores, with streetcar conductors, with people who like to talk about politics." Weir fit easily into a couple of these categories.

A lesser-known common interest of Coolidge and Weir was local politics. At that time, the Northampton City Council was made up of two bodies, the Common Council, with three representatives from each of the seven wards, and the Board of Aldermen, with one person from each ward. In 1901, Weir's short political career began when he won one of the Ward 2 Common Council seats and then the next year its seat on the Board of Aldermen. Maybe Coolidge as a Republican Party committeeman needed someone to run and convinced Weir to do his civic duty, or perhaps Weir caught the political bug from his roomer. After all, they lived together during Coolidge's fall 1898 campaign for city council. Weir did not climb higher in local politics, but he did serve as an elector under the will of Oliver Smith at Smith Charities later in that decade.

Like many of Coolidge's friends, the good-natured Weir had a sense of humor. Clifford Lyman, a clerk and later owner of the renamed Bridgman and Lyman Bookshop, devoted two *Daily Hampshire*

Gazette articles to the "Wit and Wisdom of Robert Weir" in 1936. He recounted that Weir was a rural Tennessee boy at heart, raising pigs in the meadows section of Northampton and chickens ten miles from Sacramento, California after he moved there. On a visit to Lyman's father's farm in Southampton, the older Mr. Lyman observed that there was no money in raising pigs. Weir replied that money was only in raising pigs because he had never taken any money out. Judge Henry Field, Coolidge's friend and former mentor, told Lyman that he had walked into the bookstore and discovered Weir reading. He asked him, "Aren't you working?" Weir replied, "No, the boss is away."

The Introduction

Weir, with his good social skills, seemed to know practically every Clarke School faculty member so when Coolidge asked to be introduced to a woman he had spotted from his window, Weir was able to oblige.

Grace Goodhue had graduated from the University of Vermont in 1902 and went to Clarke that fall to become a teacher of the deaf. In her autobiography, she wrote that she met Coolidge in her second year, probably meaning sometime after September 1903. One story is that Grace was watering flowers in the garden of the building next door to where she lived when she looked up and spotted Calvin shaving—wearing a hat. He heard her laughter at this strange sight and pressed Weir to make the introduction to the dark-haired, vivacious beauty. When they first met, Coolidge explained to Grace that he was anchoring a cowlick with his hat. Their first date was attending a Republican Party rally at city hall.

Grace Coolidge related one occasion when Weir was part of a double date. "Early in my acquaintance with him, Mr. Coolidge expressed a desire to make a fourth at a picnic which the steward of Clarke School, in whose house he had a room, and one of the other teachers and I were planning. I told him that we had decided that he might join us if he would provide lunch. To this he readily agreed."

On the day of the outing, after each of them had devoured two chicken sandwiches and strawberry shortcake, the picnickers did not finish all the macaroons. Coolidge asked how many each person had eaten and compared that to the number left over—there was half a macaroon missing and never found. This story is usually used to frown on Coolidge's economy and thrift.

Being a devoted spouse, Grace Coolidge retold the tale in the June 1935 *Good Housekeeping* with this spin, "Moderation in all things governed his life. In no way was his economy related to stinginess. He spent in accordance with his means, but he watched expenditures carefully and was averse to waste of any sort."

Calvin Coolidge and Grace Goodhue married on October 4, 1905 in her native Burlington, Vermont, and later after rearing two sons and holding many political offices, President Coolidge penned one of the finest, most often-quoted tributes ever written about a first lady, "For almost a quarter of a century she has borne with my infirmities, and I have rejoiced in her graces."

Losing Touch

At some point relations between Coolidge and Weir seem to have cooled. In 1935, *Good Housekeeping* magazine produced a series of articles with fifty people, major and minor characters in Coolidge's life, remembering their interactions with the former president. Weir, the man who had lived with Coolidge for more than eight years and loved to tell stories, was not among them. Perhaps he was not asked, or he was asked and declined. His obituary mentioned a long illness. He would have needed to write his reminiscences about a year and a half before his death.

Another possibility is that a distancing began in 1907 when George W. Cable forced Adelene Moffat to resign her position as secretary for women's work for the Home Culture Clubs. His stated reason was the clubs' fiscal condition. Weir may have felt that Coolidge, who was the secretary of the clubs' board at that time, should have been able to prevent the move. Coolidge had joined the board in May 1904 and participated in the board and clubs' activities when he was in town. Shortly after becoming a board member, he spoke to a men's group on the topic of "The Use of Money in Political Campaigns." In the 1907 situation, it appears that Coolidge failed to speak on Moffat's behalf, although he did not attend the first critical meeting. But on a later second vote, he went with the majority to uphold Weir's aunt's resignation. Adelene Moffat's forced departure was both very visible and very unpopular with the clubs' membership and at least one board member, who was a major source of funding and resigned as a result of the controversy.

Moffat left a job that she had essentially created. The students, especially those involved in the Women's Council, were unhappy, as was one of the city's newspapers, the *Northampton Daily Herald*, a *Gazette* rival published between 1883 and 1921. The *Gazette* took a more neutral position than the *Herald*, but both papers continued to report on the story.

The Home Culture Clubs survived this controversy. To satisfy some critics led by the *Herald*, they had an independent audit of their books, and although several board members changed over the next two years, it was mostly due to natural attrition. Coolidge remained involved, and later Grace became a board member. The name changed to The People's Institute, which is still a fixture on Gothic Street.

On July 31, 1913, Weir, by then forty years old, married Maud Cunningham, an accountant three years his senior. The ceremony was conducted by a justice of the peace in Hartford, Connecticut. By January 1914, Weir had resigned his position at Clarke School and joined the Norwood Engineering Company as a salesman. The company, established in 1893, made water purification and filtration systems for public and commercial clients as well as for swimming pools.

By September 1918, he had moved to California without his wife. On September 12 in San Diego, he named her his closest relative and gave her Northampton address on his World War I Draft Registration card. It is interesting to note that all of his brothers and sisters moved to California and died there, but they had settled in different parts of the state. Weir's move appears to have led to the equivalent of divorce by desertion, although the two continued to acknowledge that they were married. In the 1930 U.S. Census, Weir listed himself as a married man while living in Sacramento, and Maud can be found in the Northampton census rolls as a 'married, white, female'. Maud remained in Northampton and until 1934, advertised in the classifieds and was listed in the city directories as 'Maud Weir, accountant.' From 1935 to 1946, she lived at the then-named Lathrop Home for Aged and Invalid Women at 215 South Street. When Rob Weir died in 1936, Maud was alive but not mentioned in his obituary. This marital situation may have been enough to keep public figures like the Coolidges from further contact with their old friend, which would account for Weir not writing reminiscences for *Good Housekeeping*. Whatever the situation was, it was not so bad that it kept Clifford Lyman of the Bridgman Bookshop from visiting him on a trip to California.

One day, Weir started talking to a clerk in a Sacramento bookstore and was excited to discover that the young man, Eugene Bouchard, had lived in Northampton. Soon Bouchard was a resident in the rooming house run by Weir and his business partner, Louis Ardite. According to Bouchard, Weir never tired of joking and telling stories. Ardite and Weir had a building management company that at one time provided cleaning and night security for two banks.

Weir lived in Sacramento during the last seven years of his life, dying there in September 1936 after a period of poor health. Stephen Day, a manager for Crane and Company in Sacramento and another Northampton native, had persuaded Weir to go to Day's office and dictate the story of his relationship with Grace and Calvin Coolidge to a secretary there, but he died before he could do so.

A few days after news of his death reached Northampton, Clifford Lyman wrote a tribute to Weir in the *Gazette* that ended with these lines that may explain the man better than was possible before, "There is one thing I must not forget to say: Robert, like Mark Twain, had his days of depression. He used to have 'the blues' awfully. It was pathetic to see him, but they didn't last long. He would snap out of them and be more humorous than ever."

Eating at Rahar's Inn

Rahar's Inn on Old South Street opened in 1897. Coolidge was a frequent diner there, both while he roomed with Robert Weir at Clarke School and after his marriage. It was a good place to talk business and politics, as Coolidge recalled: "I took my meals at Rahar's Inn where there was much agreeable company consisting of professional and business men of the town and some professors of Smith College." Richard J. Rahar, the proprietor, recalled that a number of Amherst College graduates were patrons.

Rahar, an Irish-American Northampton native, went to work early in life. He and his older brother, Thomas, were already employed at Northampton Cutlery in 1880 at ages fourteen and eighteen. While Thomas remained at the factory most of his life, Richard became part of the city's hospitality industry. In 1893, he was a clerk at the Hampshire House hotel, and he managed the wine and billiards room at the Norwood Hotel at 31 Bridge Street in 1895. He was a successful businessman and traveled to Havana, Cuba in 1913 and Europe in 1936. He was one of the people asked to reminisce about Coolidge in the series of articles that *Good Housekeeping* published in 1935. He told two widely circulated stories; one he lamented was false and the other true.

> Only lately I heard the false story repeated. Mr. Coolidge was supposed to have ordered two drinks regularly every day—at noontime and at dinner. At that time a drink cost ten cents. One day the bartender told him that prices had gone up to fifteen cents each, or two for a quarter. Mr. Coolidge had put down a dime, as the story goes, but now he picked it up, replaced it with a quarter, and said, 'I'll be in for the other drink tonight'.
>
> That isn't so, because he never took a drink in the daytime, and very little at night. Maybe he would have a cocktail at dinner with one of his cronies, and a glass of beer throughout the course of the evening, but that was all.
>
> One night after dinner he passed the office desk as I was putting away two five-dollar gold pieces...I told him that I made a custom of giving Mrs. Rahar, for her personal use, any gold coins that came in.
>
> Two of his closest friends boarded at the inn at the same time—Ernest Hardy, a classmate, and Richard Irwin, afterward state senator, district attorney and judge. At the end of the month the three appeared together at the desk to pay their bills....Each of them [plunked] down five five-dollar gold pieces! Seventy-five dollars in gold!
>
> Yes—Mrs. Rahar got it.

Later, the Coolidge family occasionally ate Sunday supper at the Inn. Grace Coolidge recalled that her son, Calvin, Jr's., initial encounter with a finger bowl was on his first trip to Rahar's. Puzzling over the small dish with a lemon slice floating in warm water, he asked his father what it was. Hearing that it was to drink, he promptly did so.

Later generations of college students drank and partied at Rahar's. It was not unusual to be traveling as recently as the late 1990s and be asked "Is Rahar's still there?" when someone heard you lived in Northampton.

George Washington Cable

George W. Cable was born in New Orleans in 1844, and after serving in the Confederate Army, worked as a writer for the New Orleans *Picayune*. All his writings focused on life in the antebellum South, race relations, and civil rights at a time when people in that city were unwilling to deal with those issues. Because his audience, his publisher, and his friend, Mark Twain, were in the North, Cable began to consider moving there.

Cable gave a reading on January 21, 1884 in Northampton, where his host, Sidney Bridgman, owner of the bookstore, pointed out the advantages of settling in the beautiful college town. In July 1884, Cable moved his family to Simsbury, Connecticut, and then a year later, to Northampton.

In the fall and winter of 1884-1885, Cable and Twain traveled to about eighty-five cities on the lecture circuit, billed as the "Twins of Genius." When Cable reminisced at a memorial service held for Twain in November 1910, he recalled how they found a bookshop while out walking in Rochester, New York. Cable recommended that Twain buy a copy of Malory's *Morte d'Arthur* and predicted that he would love it. Cable was correct, and in 1889, Twain published *A Connecticut Yankee in King Arthur's Court*. When Twain visited Northampton and told his host about his latest project, Cable claimed to be the 'godfather' of that book, and Mark Twain agreed.

Cable continued to be a 'Southern writer', some thought the most important of his time. Several of his novels and collections of stories were written in Northampton: *Bonaventure* (1888), *The Negro Question* (1890), *John March, Southerner* (1894), *The Cavalier* (1901), and *Lovers of Louisiana* (1918).

Cable told an employee of the Home Culture Clubs that although Coolidge was quiet, he thought a lot. Cable urged him to watch Coolidge because he would hear of him later. Cable died January 30, 1925 in St. Petersburg, Florida at age 81, in the middle of Coolidge's presidency.

40 Round Hill Road

Coolidge shared Weir's quarters on the right side of this solid brick duplex on the Clarke School campus.

The brick duplex at 40 Round Hill Road is today known as Adams House. The two men lived on the right side of the two-and-one-half story home tucked behind Gawith Hall, once called Baker Hall, where Grace Goodhue lived while teaching at the school. Older maps of the area show that there was a street or lane running in front of the duplex so it was next door to Grace's residence as some biographers claim.

This contemporary photo shows the detailed brick work on the right façade of 40 Round Hill Road.

    The masonry work on the exterior is noteworthy. Three courses of bricks outline the ends of the gambrel roof at both ends and on the front gambrel dormer. A row of brick dentils lines up with the top of the windows on each floor and a simple brick row marks the window bottoms. Although the windows are rectangles, the brick opening is slightly arched at the top and the space filled with shaped wood. The front porch has elaborately turned columns and rails.

Chapter 3
Newlywed

Coolidge's personal life changed forever after Grace Goodhue arrived in the city to begin her lifelong association with Clarke School in the fall of 1902. By the spring of 1905, Coolidge knew his heart and arrived in Burlington, Vermont to ask Andrew Goodhue for his daughter's hand in marriage. Grace's mother, Lemira, had objections, and Coolidge spent a great part of the summer convincing her to let the wedding proceed instead of postponing it one year as she suggested. Calvin and Grace married in Burlington on October 4, 1905 in a small ceremony in her parents' living room.

The newlyweds took the train to Montreal for their honeymoon. Although they planned to stay two weeks, they returned to Northampton after only one. Grace wrote, "He made the amusing explanation that he was in a hurry to get back to Northampton in order to show off his prize. I knew better! It was his first [sic] political campaign which drew him." That bid for a seat on the school committee was the only race he would ever lose. In a conversation reported in Fuess's biography, Coolidge saw a Republican neighbor after the election who told him that he had voted for the Democratic candidate. When Coolidge inquired further, the man said it was because he believed school committee members should have children in the system. "Coolidge's only response was, 'Might give me time.'"

While looking for a place to live, the couple took up temporary quarters at the Norwood Hotel at 31 Bridge Street with Colonel George Keeler, proprietor. According to one biographer, the Coolidges lived for three weeks "at the Norwood, then Northampton's leading hotel, only a short distance from his office." Grace tells a slightly different version in her autobiography which is documented by some newspaper articles of the time:

> We took up temporary lodging at the Norwood hotel, which was not then a financial success…it became apparent that it was doomed to failure and it was about to close its doors. The furnishings,

including the linen and silver, were to be sold, and we took advantage of this to buy a supply sufficient for our immediate needs. For some years our sheets and pillowcases and some of our table linen were identified by the mark in indelible ink, "Norwood Hotel."

Grace said they looked at a variety of possible rentals, including the half house on Massasoit Street that later would be their long-term home before deciding to rent a furnished house from a Smith College professor.

Renting a Library of Classics

John Everett Brady taught Latin at Smith College, but in 1905 he was given sick leave beginning at the Thanksgiving recess for the rest of the academic year. Henrietta Seelye, wife of Smith College President L. Clark Seelye, recorded in her diary that Professor and Mrs. Brady left for Florida on Friday, November 3. The Coolidges rented their house at 5 Crescent Street until the third week in August 1906.

Brady had arrived with a new doctorate from Heidelberg to begin teaching at Smith in 1888 and retired in 1926. During those years, he maintained an intense enthusiasm for his subject and his students, but was known to be somewhat eccentric and to fill every available blackboard surface with illegible handwriting. Today, an annual prize for excellence bearing his name is awarded by the Smith Department of Classical Languages and Literatures.

Professor Brady retired to his beloved South and died in his native North Carolina in January 1941 after a long period of failing health.

Coolidge must have loved this house if Professor Brady left any of his books behind. In his autobiography, Coolidge said he spent his evenings while a law student reading the classics: "Some of the orations of Cicero I translated, being especially attached to the defense of his friend the poet Archias, because in it he dwelt on the value and consolation of good literature."

Coolidge read before falling asleep at night, and Grace told of the pile of books that were on his bedside table never to be disturbed. The Bible was always there plus the *Letters, Lectures, and Addresses of Charles Edward Garman*, an outstanding Amherst College philosophy professor, and two paperback volumes of *Paradise Lost*. Even when traveling, Coolidge carried the two copies of Milton's classic.

Mrs. Coolidge remembered that his library was housed in one small five-shelved oak bookcase "with a sateen curtain in front." His collection numbered about one hundred books including his college texts plus a leather-bound set of Shakespeare's plays, three Kipling novels, and a set of Hawthorne's works. Grace admitted that he seldom bought a book, although friends and writers gave him volumes until they numbered about five thousand by the time his presidential term was over. Over fifty boxes of books were stored at Forbes Library until the Coolidges found space at The Beeches, their final home.

The Norwood Hotel, 31 Bridge Street

The Norwood Hotel was at the corner of Bridge and Main Street; parts of it exist today.

The Norwood Hotel was a picture-perfect example of a white clapboard New England hotel, but behind the beautiful façade was a troubled history. When a new addition was built in 1892 at a cost of $10,000, the Gazette carefully described its newest feature—a ladies' entrance totally separate from the main entrance and leading directly to the "ladies parlor." The other public rooms on the first level included a dining room that seated over two hundred guests, a music hall, a men's reading room, and the now curiously named drummers' sample room. (Although this term for "traveling salesman" would go out of use around the time of World War I, drummers were those itinerant representatives of businesses whose enthusiasm and sometimes annoying "beating of the drum" for their products earned them the none-too-flattering name.) It had seventy bedrooms on the upper floors. The Norwood had the requisite front porch of more resort-style hotels of its time and also a tower with a three-foot boardwalk around its upper level for viewing. The large lawn was shaded with elm trees.

Newlywed   39

Mr. Bradstreet, the proprietor, had experience managing a Boston hotel so hopes were high for this establishment. In 1895, Coolidge's Amherst fraternity held a dinner there. A new proprietor was announced in December 1900, but the hotel did not thrive long before fire ravaged it in October 1901. In April 1905, Colonel Keeler, another new proprietor, reopened the establishment after a three-month renovation. The hotel was totally refurbished, and the kitchen was refitted with its first gas stove. Keeler wanted to appeal to the locals and family and business travelers. Lunches served from noon to 2:30 p.m. cost fifty cents.

The summer of 1905 was plagued with financial troubles, and the *Gazette* announced the hotel would close on Sunday, October 29 while Grace and Calvin Coolidge were still guests. According to another newspaper story, The Norwood had been closed for eighteen months when it was sold to Mrs. Lizzie Sparks in September 1907 for use as a private hospital, so it might have reopened for a short time between these two dates. In 1935, Grace recalled that the hotel was later cut into two parts, and the end where their room had been located was moved to the corner and placed on a new foundation. It had stores on the first floor and apartments above. She is referring to the wood-frame building standing today at the southeast corner of Hawley and Bridge Street. This work, done in 1910, also included creating twelve apartments in the section that remained in place.

5 Crescent Street

This shingle-style house at 5 Crescent Street was the Coolidges' first rental home as a couple.

This house is an example of the shingle style, popular in the United States between 1880 and 1900. It began in the resort communities on the New England coast and moved inland. About one in four homes of this style have gambrel roofs like this home. The Crescent Street house is one of this style's simpler forms but has many of the characteristic details beginning at the front porch with its squat, Romanesque arches. Above a brick foundation are wood clapboards on the first floor and shingles on the second and third. The roof to the east and west is punctuated with four dormers with steeply pitched roofs and a small second-floor porch to the east. There are typical window groupings on the third floor in the north and south gable ends. Today, there is about 2,200 square feet of living space on the first two floors plus a finished attic.

The Reverend Rufus Underwood purchased a large parcel of land including this lot from a carpenter, Albert G. Jewett, in 1888, and the house at the corner of Crescent and Prospect Streets was built around 1890. In 1893, Underwood sold the house to Mary Seelye Brady, the professor's wife, for $5,000 and he himself was reported living on another part of the parcel at 27 Crescent Street. On December 31, 1892, the *Springfield Republican* reported five new homes built on Crescent Street ranging in price from $4,000 to $10,000 that year. The Reverend Underwood owned the least expensive, perhaps this house or another built on his large parcel. Professor Brady bought the property from his wife in 1914 and added a lot on the Prospect Street side in 1919 that now serves as the backyard.

Chapter 4
The Settled Life

The Neighbors Who Were So Kind

Both Calvin and Grace Coolidge wrote about their love for the house at 21 Massasoit Street. She wrote with passion, saying, "For most of us there is one spot on earth which is dearer than all others. For me it is here in this little nine-room cottage, which really is only half a house and could be set into the state dining room at the White House with some space to spare.... In it both of our children were born, and it has grown dearer through the years of absence...It fits us like a comfortable well-worn garment."

Coolidge also explained the family's long tenure at this address: "We liked the house where our children came to us and the neighbors who were so kind. When we could have had a more pretentious home we still clung to it. So long as I lived there, I could be independent and serve the public without ever thinking that I could not maintain my position if I lost my office.... We lived where we did that I might better serve the people."

The couple stayed twenty-four years in this duplex, six houses from Elm Street. Here they experienced all of Calvin's major political triumphs and many of their family events. The clapboard frame structure was unique among presidential homes: a rental with two units and for these reasons not the type of home associated with state or national office holders.

Calvin talked about the moving process, which took place in August 1906, in sparse, practical terms, but always with an understated elegance: "We moved into the house in Massasoit Street that was to be our home for so long. I attended to the furnishing of it myself, and when it was ready Mrs. Coolidge and I walked over to it. In about two weeks our first boy came on the evening of September seventh."

In the Coolidge family, what to name sons was complicated or simple depending on your point of view. The names Calvin or John were given to almost all males. Calvin and Grace proudly named their firstborn John Calvin Coolidge to honor Calvin's father, Colonel John

C. Coolidge. Ironically, the future president himself had been named after the colonel and was baptized "John Calvin Coolidge," but he wrote in his autobiography that the family always called him Calvin, and the John was discarded. He may have had a different idea about his name as a young adult. For example, the four Amherst College catalogs from his era list him as "John Calvin Coolidge." He penned his name in the front of his law books in 1895 as "J. Calvin Coolidge." His first two listings in the city directories were as "John C. Coolidge, Law Student." Perhaps most telling, he signed letters to his father "J. Calvin Coolidge" until 1897. By 1898, when Coolidge began paying for a display ad in the city directory, "John" was gone again, and he was "Calvin Coolidge." At last, the couple may have put the name question to rest on April 13, 1908 at the birth of their second son, whom they named Calvin Coolidge, Jr.

Coolidge oversaw the furnishing of the house for his very pregnant wife by buying an oak bedroom set and contributing his college bookcase and books. Grace's father had built them a couch as a wedding gift, and that was in the living or front room with a Morris chair favored by Calvin. There were carpets on the floors, rocking chairs for the porch, and pictures for the walls. An upright piano was there when the children were ready for music lessons. Over the mantel, a revealing verse was framed:

> A wise old owl sat on an oak,
> The more he saw, the less he spoke;
> The less he spoke, the more he heard.
> Why can't we be like that old bird?

Grace's term 'half house' may be most descriptive of its style but not of the home's size. In addition to the president's notions of economy and service, the design and living space might also have been responsible for Coolidge's long tenure there. It had the feel of a single-family home with its two-story living space plus a basement and attic. The neighbor who lived in the other half of the house after 1918 noted that his family's duplex was as large as a typical single family on the street. At approximately 2,150 square feet, each side was larger than an average rental. The Northampton assessor's records of present-day Massasoit Street show that six of the nine single-family homes that were in the neighborhood in Coolidge's time have between 1,900 and 2,400 square feet of floor space.

While Coolidge lived in this house, nothing stopped his political progress, and his neighbors could closely observe a rising star. He served as a Massachusetts state representative in 1907 and 1908. In 1910 and 1911, he was mayor of Northampton. Then it was back to the State House to serve as a state senator between 1912 and 1915. In his last two terms, he was the senate president. In November of 1915, 1916 and 1917, he was elected lieutenant governor and then governor in 1918 and 1919.

In September 1919, the Boston City Police went on strike, propelling Coolidge onto the national stage. He took a firm stand for law and order and in a telegram to Samuel Gompers, legendary head of the American Federation of Labor, he stated, "There is no right to strike against the public safety by anybody, anywhere any time." This was one sentence in the middle of what Coolidge must have considered a long, lawyerly communication. It does not represent Coolidge's generally sympathetic concern for working people.

Coolidge was elected vice president of the United States in 1920 on a ticket headed by Warren G. Harding of Ohio. When Harding died unexpectedly on August 2, 1923, Coolidge became president. He earned a term in his own right in 1924.

Although he was nicknamed "Silent Cal," he is remembered today ironically for things he said and wrote, especially his sparse but adequate statement which effectively ended his long career when in the summer of 1927 he wrote, "I do not choose to run for President in nineteen twenty eight." His last day in the White House was March 4, 1929.

Two of Coolidge's "kind" neighbors wrote about life on the same street with the famous family. Professor Elihu Grant lived at 24 Massasoit with his wife and daughter from 1908 to 1917, and Dr. Frederic Plummer, his wife, son, and daughter shared the duplex with the Coolidges from 1918 to 1930. With only a one-year gap, the two sets of continuous observations are remarkably similar, but Grant saw a less busy, less famous person so told more personal, human anecdotes. Dr. Plummer saw less of the president and more of his family, but none the less had many things to say about the Calvin Coolidge he knew.

In the winter of 1924, soon after Coolidge had suddenly become president, Professor Grant was asked to share his experiences on Massasoit Street with the employees of the W. T. Grant Company, founded and owned by his brother. The Grants moved into their home across the street just before Calvin Coolidge, Jr. was born. He described a pleasant area of families in the same stage of life where the women were friends, the men enjoyed talking with one another, and the children played happily together. Grant remembers living near other Smith College professors like himself as well as the postmaster, the Methodist minister, and several businessmen. Grace Coolidge remembered her children's friends as two sons of the family doctor, one son of a railroad engineer, and another of a manufacturer. Except for the friend on active duty with the Navy, three of the former playmates were in John Coolidge's wedding party and two of them served as pall bearers at Grace's funeral.

Grant took some interest in his front yard and remembered getting timely advice and comment from Coolidge. "He would sometimes come across and look at the little spruces which I had set out on the lawn. He was particularly apt to note the new growth.... Once I was clumsily learning to swing a scythe when he came over and helped me learn the motion."

Coolidge had plenty of experience using a scythe during years on his father's Vermont farm.

Professor Grant may have needed help with these practical gardening matters. His brother, the retail giant William T. Grant, describes him as "a brilliant student, the valedictorian of his class and who went on to become a minister and, in later years, a distinguished archeologist and a professor at both Smith and Haverford College." Ordained a Methodist clergyman in 1900, the professor became a member of the Society of Friends in 1911 while living on Massasoit Street, although his association with this group had begun ten years earlier while he was working as superintendent of the American Friends Schools in Ramallah and Jerusalem. At Smith College, he was a professor of biblical literature. After moving to Haverford, he broadened his work to include archaeology, and he led four excavations to a site in Palestine. One colleague recalled that he was always sympathetic to his Arab workers and neighbors, a trait that set him apart from most other archaeologists of the time.

W. T. Grant sought Coolidge's legal advice when in Northampton to visit his brother and sister-in-law, who were Calvin and Grace's neighbors. L – R: Professor Elihu Grant, Almy Grant, William T. Grant.

On one occasion when W. T. Grant was in Northampton to visit his brother, he needed legal advice about a store lease. His first store had opened in 1906 in Lynn, Massachusetts, and in the first ten years, he expanded to thirty-six locations. When he died in 1972 at age ninety-six, there were 1,200 stores. At the time of that visit to Northampton, he still did most of the real estate work himself. His brother suggested he consult with Calvin Coolidge, who was then in the state legislature. After about an hour's discussion, Grant was ready to leave and asked about the fee. "A dollar and a half wouldn't be too much, would it?" was the reply. Coolidge had made another friend. Years later, W. T. Grant was still amazed that advice from a future president could be such a bargain.

Professor Grant had observed Coolidge's physical and mental characteristics. He was "tall, spare, dignified, taciturn" and youthful in appearance. He was distinguished from other politicians by his capacity for hard work, his well-thought-out positions, and his ability to attract Democratic votes without any of the usual personality traits of a politician. While other politicians had their ups and downs, people had steadfast confidence in Coolidge, and he never lost the respect of his constituents. He had his objective clearly in mind and persistently pursued it.

Professor Grant said that Coolidge's 'Yankee' personality was not hard to understand. There were many men of his type "in the law, in the ministry and other professions, in business and in the town meetings. The remarkable thing about Mr. Coolidge is that he has so many of the characteristics of the type and that he has them in such perfect blend. Patience, efficiency and self-control are joined in him…His greatest fun is doing his duty." Grant found him very observant, "one who said very little but said enough."

Frederic Plummer, who enjoyed raising roses, also mentioned the Coolidges' garden and the president's personality in six articles he wrote for the *Boston Globe* in 1930, just after the Coolidges had moved to their next home. He remembered Grace's efforts in the garden and those of the Coolidge family housekeeper, Alice Reckahn. When he first saw his half of the house, Mrs. Coolidge had planted a row of flowers along his side as well as hers. The previous tenants, Elizabeth Prindle, a widow, and her daughter, Imogene, may have moved, leaving the right side vacant for a time, giving Grace an opening to expand her garden or simply unify the appearance of the front and sides of the house.

Mrs. Reckahn and Grace shared duties in the vegetable garden in the back, and its bounty with the neighbors. The garden existed until the White House pets took over the yard in 1929. The two Coolidge boys planted pine trees on the Massasoit Street property that their mother moved to their next home on Hampton Terrace. To Grace's disappointment, the trees had grown too large to move to her next home on Ward Avenue. They remain today at 20 Stearns Court, a lot severed from the property after the Coolidge era.

Grace and her sons took being good neighbors seriously. The Plummers' first visitors on Massasoit Street were the Coolidge boys, followed two days later by Grace herself. After the president spent more time fishing, Grace kept the neighbors supplied with the excess catch. Plummer also revealed that often extra flowers were distributed to institutions and neighbors.

By the time the Plummers moved to the street, Coolidge was already lieutenant governor so he had less time for neighborliness. Plummer claimed that he did not know who lived in the other half of the house or even that the lieutenant governor lived in Northampton when he rented 19 Massasoit. In the end, he said that he could not imagine better neighbors with whom to share these peculiar circumstances. People rang the Plummers' doorbell mistakenly looking for Coolidge and sometimes asking him if Coolidge would mind if they took a picture of the house. Some people actually thought Plummer was the president although the resemblance was little or none according to the inhabitant of 19 Massasoit.

Coolidge was the most reticent man Plummer ever met but he felt it was his neighbor's own temperament that was the biggest barrier to knowing him. Having grown up in a small New England town himself, Plummer felt he knew what to expect from Coolidge, who he, like Professor Grant, felt had the pure 'Yankee' personality, perhaps to a fault. Coolidge's dignity accounted for Plummer never hearing anybody call him Cal, never seeing him in his shirtsleeves or never having more than an hour's worth of conversation with him in the twelve years they were sharing the same house. Plummer was a Democrat but voted for his neighbor because he had confidence that Coolidge was so shrewd that he would never be taken in by politicians.

Frederic W. Plummer, principal of Northampton High School, lived at 19 Massasoit Street beginning in 1918.

While confirming that Coolidge was indeed careful with money, Plummer noted that "if all of the Northampton people who have been beneficiaries of his assistance in time of need or have received legal advice free of charge would testify, an unsuspected aspect of the Coolidge character would be revealed." It seems Coolidge had priorities for his spending. He said his accomplishments during two years as mayor of Northampton were three: lowering taxes, paying off part of the debt, and giving teachers a raise. The stereotype of his pecuniary ways persisted outside of Northampton through the entire presidency and after. In February 1929, at a dinner given by a cabinet officer just before the president was to leave office, there was a lot of angling for information about Coolidge's plans in retirement. The president said little but smiled broadly when the hostess suggested that he become a professor of thrift at Aberdeen University.

There were several instances in which people other than W. T. Grant reported free or nearly free legal advice from Coolidge, but most telling are the reports of financial generosity to people he knew. Ralph Hemenway, Coolidge's law partner, recalled that when he was short of cash because of a local bank closing, the former president came into his office and put a check for $5,000 on the blotter. Coolidge told Hemenway he could have more—as much as he needed—as he turned and walked back into the adjoining office.

Clifford H. Lyman, the local historian, gave a note he had received from Coolidge to the Reverend Albert J. Penner soon after the young minister at the Edwards Church had presided at the ex-president's funeral. The note said, "Dear Mr. Lyman: I am enclosing a small check

The door to Coolidge's 59 Main Street office is shown as it appeared sometime after his death in 1933.

for the church with the hope that the treasury may warrant giving a like sum to our pastor, without disclosing that I had anything to do about it. Calvin Coolidge" Penner realized this explained the anonymous fifty-dollar bill that had appeared at Christmastime, and he observed in his diary that the note revealed a little-noticed side of Coolidge.

Dr. Frederic W. Plummer was born in Maine and attended West Point. After two years, he decided not to make the army his career and returned to Maine to graduate from Bates College. He taught or was the administrator in school districts in Maine and Massachusetts before he was appointed principal of the Northampton High School, a post he held for nineteen years. Throughout his life, he was active in the Boy Scouts and was an expert in butterflies and moths. He was also a trustee of Forbes Library and first president of the Northampton Rotary Club. After his retirement, he became a member of the school committee.

Another hobby was more unusual. When he retired, at the mandatory age of seventy, it was reported that he was responsible for sixty young men attending West Point or Annapolis. He might have taken the most pride in his own son, Thomas, who graduated from Northampton High in 1921, just three years after arriving in the city. With no political connections, Dr. Plummer went to talk to his neighbor, who had just become vice president. A vice president had two chances to appoint a cadet during his four-year term. He asked Coolidge to consider Thomas for one of the appointments, if it would cause him no embarrassment. Coolidge did not promise anything, saying he had many good candidates to consider. So the Plummer family hardly dared hope that West Point was in Thomas's future, and he made plans to enter Massachusetts Institute of Technology. However, a letter of acceptance arrived with Coolidge's appointment, and Thomas graduated from the U.S. Military Academy in 1926.

Another person Plummer influenced was General Creighton W. Abrams, born in Springfield, Massachusetts in 1914 and raised across the Connecticut River in Agawam. Abrams was class president and captain of the football team, but his family circumstances made college impossible without a scholarship for tuition, room, board, and books. He was inspired after hearing Plummer speak and graduated from the

U.S. Military Academy in 1936. From 1968 to 1972, he was commander of U.S. military operations in Vietnam and then Army Chief of Staff until his death in 1974.

The duplex was not empty most of the time the Coolidges were in Washington. Lemira Goodhue, Grace's mother, lived in the half house after her husband died in April 1923. She was hospitalized in December 1927 and never discharged. She died at Northampton's Cooley Dickinson Hospital in October 1929. Her health weighed heavily on her daughter's mind during the last White House year. Grace replied to a note from Professor Grant's wife, Almy Chase Grant, in June 1928 saying that she felt that she was off on a great adventure at the designated

Lemira Goodhue, Grace Coolidge's mother, lived at 21 Massasoit Street after she was widowed in 1923 and before she was hospitalized for her last illness late in 1927.

summer White House in Wisconsin. "The only drawback is the distance from Northampton and mother but I can make the trip in thirty-six hours and we must consider the President's needs first."

Calvin Coolidge did not have the warmest of relationships with his mother-in-law, but the neighbors seemed to like her very much. Grace Coolidge related a tale about Professor Grant paying a call on them one Sunday afternoon. The Coolidges plus Mrs. Goodhue were on their front porch. Grant began telling stories of his experiences in Palestine, and Mrs. Goodhue was a good listener. The session lasted until twilight, but Calvin had excused himself earlier. Mother Goodhue tried to bring Coolidge up-to-date later that evening, and Grace remembered hearing him mumble from behind a newspaper, "He's used to talking to the heathen."

Dr. Plummer and his wife, Mellie, got to know and like Mrs. Goodhue. He called her a "natural-born neighbor, like her daughter." She gave her neighbors a firsthand account of the inauguration ceremonies in March 1925 after her first trip to Washington, D.C. An avid reader, she took an interest in current events. She took walks along Elm Street with the Boston terrier, Beans, a gift to the president that the first couple passed on to Mrs. Goodhue. When the Plummers got a similar dog, Grace urged them to name their pet Pork, so the house would have Pork and Beans.

It takes a community to support a wife and two children while a husband works out of town, and the Massasoit neighborhood set a fine example during Coolidge's years in Boston. He was gone from his family a great deal of the time during those years, leaving by train on Monday morning and returning on Friday evening. They had a live-in housekeeper from about 1916 onward—Alice Reckahn, a widow, who did most household chores.

While Professor Grant and Dr. Plummer observed, Grace went about making at least one deep friendship that allowed the family to function during his absences, since she did not drive or even own a car. Mrs. Reuben B. (Therese) Hills, who lived at 69 Massasoit Street, picked Grace up for daily food shopping in her car. Mr. Hills was the owner of the brassworks in the nearby village of Haydenville, and later he was one of the honorary pall bearers at the former president's funeral. During the Washington years, Therese spent a lot of time in the White

House keeping Grace company. "Hillsy" was born Therese Christiansen in Larvik, Norway in 1885. She visited Grace's mother in the hospital regularly and reported to the first lady by letter. The White House physician, Dr. Boone, spoke to Mrs. Goodhue's doctor several times a week and gave Grace medical updates, but Hillsy's personal assessment was important to Grace.

There was little that Mrs. Hills would not do if asked and no one was happier with the prospect of having Grace back in Northampton than she was. She supplied the president with his favorite chocolates from home, which he playfully blamed for a weight gain in 1929. In late February 1929 as the Coolidges prepared for their move back to Northampton, Hillsy received a detailed letter about the eleven crates and boxes that Grace had asked the movers to take to the Hills's home for temporary storage. Some contained fruit that would freeze and spoil if left in the barn so the first lady requested that her friend find room in her basement.

The twenty-second birthday celebration for John Coolidge, which Therese Hills organized, is a good example of the ongoing community support. In 1928, John was with his parents at the summer White House in Brule, Wisconsin, but needed to go back to the Northeast to start a job with the New York, New Haven and Hartford Railroad before his birthday on September 7. He stopped in Northampton and ate a dinner prepared by the housekeeper, Mrs. Reckahn, while she told him about his grandmother's health. Later, he went to see the Hillses, whose son, Jack, had been a friend since childhood and a classmate at Amherst College. The next night he ate with the Brown family around the corner on Elm Street. Dr. Edward Brown was the president's Northampton doctor. His son, Steve, was John's Amherst College roommate. Later it was Jack Hills, and Steve Brown and his brother, Richard, who were in John Coolidge's wedding party. The next evening Mrs. Hills threw a birthday party for John.

After returning to Northampton from the White House in March 1929, the former president could not sit and rock on his front porch without people staring, and he and his wife had no room to entertain out-of-town guests. The couple needed a larger lawn for the dogs that were used to roaming the entire White House lawn. Dr. Plummer counted one car every six seconds passing the house one Sunday afternoon in early

The Coolidges adored their pets, which they brought back from the White House in March 1929. (Photo by Eric Stahlberg)

1930. The home's size was a problem foreseen in the winter of 1929 when the president wrote to Therese Hills asking her to measure the rooms in the half house to see if a rug acquired in Washington measuring 18½ by 11 feet could be used in any room. It would not fit, as Coolidge had suspected. The small size—inside and out—and the lack of privacy resulted in the Coolidges needing new quarters so they moved to The Beeches in May 1930.

19-21 Massasoit Street

The duplex at 19-21 Massasoit Street is a large, wood-framed New England home with wood clapboard siding and a hipped roof. Painted traditional white for many years, it is now gray. It was yellow with maroon trim in 1976 when it was placed on the National Register of Historic Places.

James W. O'Brien, a local businessman, built the house in 1900-1901 and after 1918, owned it as well, according to the National Register nomination. He was in partnership with E .T. Barrett as a builder and developer while they also maintained an insurance and real estate office at 106 Main Street. Mr. Barrett gave his name to Barrett Place and Barrett Street. Another of their projects was developing the area of streets across Route 9 from Trinity Park in Florence, such as Plymouth and Sumner Avenues. Coolidge often served as their lawyer.

The interior spaces at 19 and 21 Massasoit Street were mirror images of each other, but on the exterior, the front porches were not

The front porch was Coolidge's favorite spot at 21 Massasoit Street, where the family rented half of the large duplex for 24 years.

exactly alike. The Coolidge's former porch at number 21 is gabled and the one to the right at number 19 has a flat roof that wraps around and becomes the roof for its front bay window. In 1920 when Coolidge was nominated for U.S. vice president, a Notification Day ceremony took place that began on Massasoit Street and ended at Smith College. The photographs of the festivities show that the porch roof's flat surfaces were surrounded by a wood railing creating a second-floor porch.

The Coolidge front porch is well known because the president liked to sit there in a rocking chair and smoke a cigar. Early photographs show him partially shielded by vines, but later images show a fully exposed area with no protection from curious eyes.

Inside were a living room, dining room, entry hall and kitchen on the first floor, with three bedrooms and a bath on the second plus stairs to an attic. The National Register nomination described the interior of 21 Massasoit in detail:

> The main entrance on the Coolidge side leads into a three foot square vestibule, which provides access to the main entry room. From this room a wide archway opens into the front parlor, which has a hexagonal bay window and a Doric pilastered mantel. A similar archway at the rear of the main entry room opens onto the dining room, where the exterior wall is graced by a low window seat. Triangular shaped pantries fill both corners of the room, while an enclosed service hall passes to the right of the dining room and connects the main entrance to the kitchen in the rear.

There was an open staircase to the second floor with its three bedrooms and one bath. The stairs continue to the next floor, which has two storage rooms and another bedroom. On the other side, Dr. Plummer used this room, which he called unfinished, as a home office, but the Coolidges did not say how they used their room.

The house has remained a residence through the years except for its short time as the "Calvin Coolidge Memorial Tea Room." It opened in October 1935 with some furniture loaned to the proprietors by Grace Coolidge herself, but it closed less than a year later on August 21, 1936.

Chapter 5
The Best Home for the Coolidges

Building The Beeches

Three men are responsible for designing, building, and paying for what was to date the most impressive house in Northampton, The Beeches. On April 23, 1914, a contract to construct a home on Hampton Terrace was signed by Professor Henry Noble MacCracken, known as "Noble," and Frank L. Huxley, a well-regarded Northampton builder, in the presence of Richard H. Dana, a New York City architect. The total cost was to be $18,867. In the end, the cost was close to ten percent more, or about $20,500. The majority of the increase came when a two-car detached garage was added to the plans.

MacCracken graduated with a bachelor's and a master's degree from New York University where his father, Henry Mitchell MacCracken, was the long-time chancellor. He received his doctorate at Harvard in 1907 and went to Oxford the next year. After returning and teaching a short time at Harvard, he was appointed Professor of English at the Sheffield Scientific School at Yale.

When MacCracken was appointed Professor of English at Smith College in mid-September 1913, he came to Northampton from New Haven without his wife and family less than a week before the college opened. As he started his new position, he looked for suitable housing, a search made all the more difficult because he still maintained a full fall-semester teaching schedule at Yale. He did not try to postpone starting his position at Smith because he needed a life change. That year the MacCrackens had lost their firstborn son and also one of Professor MacCracken's brothers.

By mid-October, he reported to Smith's President Burton that he had been unable to find any house that would be desirable for more than one semester. Renting on that basis would involve the work and expense of moving twice, so he arranged with his Smith department chair to continue living in New Haven, Connecticut through the winter and to teach at Smith Mondays through Wednesdays. MacCracken also had a personal reason for this request. His wife was pregnant and having a difficult time so they preferred not moving away from her doctor or moving during the winter.

On December 26, he wrote to President Burton again with the problem solved. He told Burton that he would buy land from Miss Harriet Clapp at the corner of Munroe Street and Hampton Terrace since his wife really favored designing and building a house. It was not just Marjorie Dodd MacCracken who had this dream. Her husband recalled: "Whenever we went on a train, pencil and paper came out and we planned our house. In seven years we had worked it out." Estimating that the location was about a ten-minute walk to the campus, he emphasized his first impressions of a good view, a large grove of trees, and two springs. Perhaps MacCracken felt the need to promote the site to President Burton because most professors lived in the Ward 2 streets around the college. The professor said his lot was "in the unfashionable part of town across the brook."

MacCracken's wife and their daughter, nicknamed Maisry, moved to nearby Amherst where their second daughter, Joy, was born on May 27, 1914.

The sale closed in mid-January 1914 for an undisclosed amount. At this time, the *Daily Hampshire Gazette* reported that landscape gardeners had already inspected the property and were working on the design for the driveway, tennis court, and shrubbery. The house was to be designed by Murphy and Dana, architects working in New York City. On July 30, 1914, MacCracken bought a further 6,500 square feet of property from Miss Clapp referred to as Lot 11, Sumner Avenue. A large involved project was planned, one that the MacCrackens might not have undertaken had they known that they would only live there a short time.

MacCracken, his wife, and children hoped to move into their home around October 1, but construction was delayed, and they waited "impatiently" in rental rooms in Northampton. They had moved into the unfinished house by December when his appointment as Vassar College president was announced to both student bodies and the press. "Mercifully, too, [The Beeches] was minus a telephone and a doorbell, and people left us alone after finding Marjorie and me in work clothes unpacking," he recounted. The last bills for the initial building costs were sent on January 1, 1915 just a month before MacCracken took office at Vassar, a position he held until 1946. His last day at Smith was January 27, 1915. The MacCrackens spent some money during the next three years in further improvements, but Huxley's records show that it was less than a hundred dollars per year. During this time, they spent summers in the house. MacCracken was an educational liberal and always believed that women's colleges were more fortunate than men's because they established their traditions by starting from scratch. He began his long association with women's institutions by teaching at Smith for three semesters followed by a thirty-one year tenure as president of Vassar College. According to his obituary, MacCracken's liberal philosophy caused him difficulty during his first month in Poughkeepsie, because he openly supported a burning issue of the day—women's suffrage. He was fired for being too liberal three years later, but he was rehired after the students, faculty, and three trustees protested. He was also an advisor to the founder and then president of the board of trustees of Sarah Lawrence College.

The second group involved in the building of The Beeches was the architectural firm of Murphy and Dana, with offices in New York and later China. The firm closed in 1921 after fourteen years in partnership. Richard Henry Dana III, the designer of the house, was a part-time professor of architecture at Yale beginning in 1908 so he may have met MacCracken there. Dana's father wrote the book *Two Years Before the Mast*. His partner, Henry Killam Murphy, was an 1899 graduate of Yale. The firm designed residences and commercial buildings, and later theaters and educational buildings in the Northeast.

In 1914, at about the same time Dana was designing the MacCracken house, Murphy was invited to work on the Changsha (Hunan) Yale-in-China medical campus. He took the first of many trips to East Asia, where the firm established a Shanghai office. Continuing to work there into the 1930s, he designed buildings that tried to blend elements of northern Chinese architecture with modern Western materials and construction techniques.

Ironically, Murphy designed one college that had a Northampton connection, the Ginling College for Women. Three academic buildings and three dormitories were planned and then completed in 1923. The Social and Athletic Building, a gift of the alumnae of Smith College, Ginling's sister college, was flanked by a science building and a recitation building. By 1924, Smith was the largest contributor among the eleven U.S. mission boards and institutions that supported Ginling. During the 1924–1925 academic year, the alumnae association tried to raise $1,500 for the Chinese institution. The National Ginling University was formed in 1951 with the merger of Ginling College and the University of Nanking.

The third member of The Beeches team was the builder, Frank L. Huxley, a second-generation contractor who learned the business from his father, John. When Frank died suddenly of a heart attack in June 1928 at age fifty-eight, his obituary noted that he had been a contractor for about twenty-five years. However, he was listed as a carpenter as early as the 1889–1890 city directory. The *Gazette* was glowing in its praise for this man, who had also built the paper's new building at 16 Armory Street the summer before. He had a large woodworking shop and lived at 46 Franklin Street, after many years on Arlington Street.

In September 1919, Professor MacCracken sold his dream house to Morris L. Comey, holding a mortgage of $18,000 at five and a half percent for five years. The discharge was recorded on June 16, 1925, two months after Mr. Comey's death.

The Beeches is arguably the best residence in Northampton. Professor MacCracken saw that "upon the beech bark every pair of lovers for a hundred years had carved their initials, and 'The Tryst' was the inevitable name." The second owners, the Comeys, gave it the more dignified name by which it has been known ever since.

Reports at the time of the Coolidges' purchase gave some idea about what the first two owners passed on to the former first couple, and a brochure printed when Grace Coolidge was selling it in the 1930s adds further detail. The shingled exterior was painted to match the leaf color of the numerous beech trees and the window trim was another subtle shade of green. The gabled copper roof gradually aged so its patina blended with the foliage. The first floor had a foyer, library with built-in bookcases, 18- by 30-foot living room with fireplace, dining room, kitchen, and half bath. Ceilings on the first floor were linen and the walls, Japanese grass cloth. The second floor had four bedrooms—

one with a fireplace, two baths, and a dressing room. The third floor had two bedrooms, a bath, and a billiard room "richly appointed." Grace was willing to sell the billiard table and equipment with the house. There was an enclosed porch off the living room and two sleeping porches on the second floor.

MacCracken remembered some interesting details about the construction. While digging the foundation, workers found the tusk of a narwhal at a depth of six feet. "Winding paths led down to the meadows, where we set a wading pool for little Maisry, fed by a tiny spring." The college superintendent/gardener, Edward Canning, designed the gardens and a tennis court.

The son of the owners after the Coolidges, Sidney P. Bailey, remembered that he and his younger brother found many items that set the house apart from a typical Northampton dwelling when they took residency—a small elevator, front and back doorbells, a floor bell in the dining room, a wall bell in the living room at the sunroom doorway, and five intercoms. "My mother soon became quite annoyed with us

The unpretentious front and side of The Beeches gave nothing away about the grand views seen from the living room and dining room at the rear.

for our constant use of the bell and intercom system to request food and drink and use of the elevator for their delivery. She…cut all but the front door bell wires and boarded up the elevator." Bailey believed that the Comeys put in the large concrete swimming pool at the bottom of the hill where the meadows began, but since the Coolidges never used it, the pool was overgrown and deteriorated so the Baileys had it removed.

A Modest Place

Elsa Comey stood between the chief of police and a state trooper who had tried to turn away the curious since the announcement. In the few days since she had sold her home to the Coolidges, she must have questioned her decision to stay there after the closing to pack and clean up. Reporters and the public tried to get a look at the house. Mrs. Comey estimated that fifty cars per hour were trying to enter the driveway of the estate, causing a true traffic jam on her quiet side street.

The national press followed the former president and first lady closely—they were celebrities in their era. Hoping to discourage the curiosity that had plagued the family since they had come home to Northampton in March 1929, Coolidge communicated on April 1, 1930 that he had purchased a "modest place with a little land." That was the former president's understated way of saying that the property had more than six acres with a very large house near the center of town. Although he went further to describe the rooms and the grounds, by April 4 Mrs. Comey was so harassed by people trying to enter the estate that with the help of law enforcement, she led a tour for fourteen reporters representing news organizations in Boston, Worcester, Springfield, New York, Washington, and Hartford plus the local press. The Coolidges announced that they would move on May 15 in hopes the press might leave Mrs. Comey alone until then.

The sale of the house and her move marked the end of a five-year period since her husband, Morris L. Comey, had died suddenly of a heart attack on April 26, 1925. He was only forty-five years old and a self-made man. Born in the New Bedford area, in 1902 he came with his wife to Easthampton, where he was employed at the West Boylston Company, a cotton manufacturing mill, with plants in both communities. About eight years before his death, he had steadily worked his way up to superintendent. After that promotion, he was one of the youngest men in such a position in the country.

It is possible to observe the large house from the street, its setback giving the promise of privacy. The reporters discovered that it was only upon entering the house that a spectacular view of mountains, meadows, and the Connecticut River was evident through the east-facing windows. Mrs. Comey's tour was comprehensive and showed that her heart was not detached yet from the property as she pointed out all the improvements that she and her husband had made during their tenure. The Comeys traveled extensively and brought furnishings from London and Damascus. One was a mid-eastern bronze censer converted to a light for the library. The couple logged at least six trips to Puerto Rico and the Panama Canal Zone alone between 1914 and 1925. When Mrs. Comey left The Beeches in May 1930 her plans included spending time with family in Fairhaven, Massachusetts and sailing to Germany to take a course in 'psychiatry'. She contemplated returning to a life of social work in New York City.

As the move came closer, Coolidge sent a letter to the local representative of a newsreel company asking him not to film the event. Reasoning that he was no longer a public figure, the former president objected to having his private affairs put on the screen. However, according to the May 14, 1930 edition of the *Gazette*, he offered to let the photographer come to the house after they were settled: "Mrs. Coolidge and I will try to help you out." On May 16, the movers began by taking the items that had been stored in the Gleason Brothers warehouse on Pearl Street for more than a year. The Coolidges came back to Northampton with sixteen trunks and 150 assorted boxes, crates, and barrels. They had come to the White House with only eight trunks, causing the president to remark: "It is easier to get into the White House than out of it." Michael J. Gleason and five assistants began moving things from Massasoit Street on Saturday, May 17 and were scheduled to take the last load on Monday.

The press had speculated since Coolidge left the White House that he would buy a property larger and more private than 21 Massasoit Street. On March 6, 1929, the *New York Times* published two rumors said to be circulating in Northampton at the time. One was that he had almost concluded negotiations for a home at 281 Elm Street, a large reproduction colonial set back from the street in a grove of trees and with a large backyard. If true, the Coolidges must have thought twice about being on such a main road. Although it would have given them the interior space they craved and added privacy from being set back on a large lot, the broad road would have encouraged, not hindered, the curious in their cars. The other rumor concerned The Beeches, but old friends of the couple said that they doubted that the Coolidges would buy such a "pretentious" house. It is hard to imagine a large home on a private lot and on a quiet street that could have better met the Coolidges' needs.

The *Gazette* analyzed the significance of the purchase by calling it the greatest compliment the ex-president could pay the city. "It shows that Mr. Coolidge did not come back here only to remain a year or so and then take up his residence in a larger city or on the Plymouth, Vermont farm. By becoming a property owner here, he indicates that Northampton is the place in which he prefers to settle down, despite the climate of California or Florida, both of which he recently visited."

At The Beeches, the Coolidges lived on a grander scale than their fellow citizens. But Grace especially enjoyed the simple things in life like the Christmas holidays and walking to do her shopping. On Christmas Eve 1930, the Young People's Forum of the First and Edwards Churches caroled at The Beeches. One of the members wrote the following verse printed in the January 2, 1931 *Gazette*:

> As Christmas carols were floating through the air,
> The door of the Beeches opened wide.
> There stood our lady with a happy smile and a cheery hello:-
> "I wish I were going to sing carols with you. Thanks and goodbye.
> A Merry Christmas, too. Oh, just a moment." And out she ran
> Just like a child in a spirit of fun,
> To share with us her Christmas treat—
> The most delicious chocolates—all one could eat.
> Then she stood by the door with her welcoming smile,
> And joined in our song of mother and child.
> I thought as the moon beamed on her face
> None could smile like that, none but Grace.
>
> R. L. F.

Coolidge was occupied by writing a two-hundred word daily column for a newspaper syndicate for one year beginning July 1, 1930. It was titled "Calvin Coolidge Says." He served as a trustee of Amherst College, as a director of the New York Life Insurance Company, and as president of the American Antiquarian Society in Worcester, Massachusetts.

Coolidge also kept regular hours at his law office in the Masonic Building at 25 Main Street. He usually arrived there at 8 a.m. and came home for lunch, returned to the office, and was home again by 6 p.m. He had a car and driver then. The Coolidges had purchased the Lincoln they had used in Washington, D.C. and hired John Bukosky, a man reported to be as quiet as his boss. Although only twenty-one or two at that time, Bukosky already had driven a Smith College professor for three years, and he stayed in Grace's employ after the president died. In the morning, he took care of the furnace then drove the president on the two roundtrips to his office and back. He took Mrs. Coolidge shopping or to see her mother at the hospital in the last months of her life. Taking care of the house and yard was his other duty.

On the morning of January 5, 1933, Coolidge went to the office although he had taken baking soda for an attack of indigestion before he left home. By 10 a.m., he told his driver to take him home, but talked briefly to Grace, who was leaving to shop downtown, and to someone in the basement shoveling coal. At noon, he went upstairs to his bedroom where Grace found him dead of heart failure a few minutes later.

Henry P. Field summed up the feelings of many Northamptonites in his tribute published in the *Gazette* on the day of Coolidge's funeral, January 7, 1933:

> His death comes as a grievous personal loss...He filled all of his main public offices to the entire satisfaction of the people. They trusted him. They felt that in his hands their government was safe. His life has been of infinite value to this country, and the nation knows the seriousness of its loss. But to us at home the loss is more intimate. In all the long history of this good city, he was its most distinguished citizen, and here in his home town, he made life better and finer for everyone who came under his influence.

Mrs. Coolidge spent little time at The Beeches after the president's death. In 1934, she began spending winters in North Carolina at the home of her friend Florence Adams. In its November 5, 1935 edition, the *Gazette* reported that the house was boarded up for a second winter. At about this time, Mrs. Coolidge dismissed her three servants and chauffeur. In February 1936, the Associated Press had a story that The Beeches was for sale and noted its bleak appearance not just from its boarded-up windows but from an eight-foot wire fence topped by barbed wire that Grace had installed to protect herself from nosy tourists after Calvin's death. When it sold in 1938, The Beeches had been empty those two years while Grace lived with Mrs. Adams in her home at 112 Washington Avenue. It was across the street from Grace's future home, Road Forks, at 11 Ward Avenue.

Grace Coolidge sold The Beeches for an undisclosed amount to Mary P. Bailey, wife of Sidney A. Bailey, a lumber company owner, in a deed dated and recorded May 2, 1938. Speculation about the sale had begun about two weeks earlier on April 20, when the newspaper erroneously reported that the sale had already taken place. The article said it was first denied by Attorney Ralph Hemenway, Calvin's former law partner and also Grace's lawyer, but was later confirmed by the attorney and the buyers. There was a rumor that Grace had given the buyers a very good financial deal, but no dollar amount is given on the deed.

Sidney P. Bailey, the son of the new owners, found out about the purchase when reporters called his college fraternity house to get a statement. He knew nothing about it and could not contact his parents by phone. He did find his grandparents, Mr. and Mrs. Frederick Starkweather, who confirmed the news and said that his parents had left town to avoid the publicity and phone calls.

Sidney and Mary Bailey had lived near The Beeches at 34 Columbus Avenue with their three sons and were friends as well as neighbors of the Coolidges. Mr. Bailey was part of the Northampton delegation that attended Coolidge's Presidential Inauguration in 1925. The two couples talked about politics, and the former president mentored Mary Bailey, who became a Republican State Committeewoman from western Massachusetts and was a delegate to every presidential nominating convention from 1932 to 1948. In 1924 during the Coolidge presidency, the Republican National Committee had welcomed its first female members.

The Baileys' son said his mother and Grace Coolidge worked together to register women voters. Calvin Coolidge supported giving women the right to vote and was governor when the Woman's Suffrage Amendment arrived in the Commonwealth for ratification by the legislature. Although he made no formal recommendation at the time, Coolidge said that he had always voted for women's suffrage and hoped it would be voted on favorably.

Conclusion

Whenever Calvin Coolidge is mentioned, certain stereotypes invariably come to mind—quiet, if not silent; frugal, if not miserly; dignified, if not wooden. His detractors used those second adjectives, but the American people were not fooled. Coolidge was a media darling. His pithy comments created great 'sound bites' decades before that phrase was invented. Often the people associated with his housing had the personal traits that he was said to be lacking—charm, charisma, and social grace.

Homes in many ways reflect their inhabitants. In the case of Calvin Coolidge, he chose modest dwellings until after the presidency, when his reputation was secure, his needs were clearly defined, and his finances in the best of shape. Coolidge's housing ranged from humble rooms to a desirable mansion with a view. The people he encountered in connection with his homes ranged similarly from a shoemaker to a college professor.

What his landlords and neighbors thought of him during his first ten years in the city is unknown except for Rhoda Lavake's already mentioned assessment that he was quiet and neat and Richard Rahar's comments about his drinking habits and sense of humor. Elihu Grant and Frederic Plummer, two of his neighbors on Massasoit Street, present the best evidence we have of his character from the 'housing' sources. Together they paint a more nuanced picture, with Grant being more positive about Coolidge's personality and Plummer leaning to the silent and wooden description of the man. On the other hand, Plummer tried to dispel the stereotype regarding Coolidge's thrift and said he could not imagine living in a similar situation with easier neighbors.

What Coolidge thought of these people is harder to discern. He made no mention of the first two rentals with the Lavakes and the Lymans in his autobiography, which may be a statement in itself. He mentions living with the steward of Clarke School but not Rob Weir by name or with any further description of him. When it comes to Massasoit Street, however, he stated that he and Grace did not want to move away from the congenial neighbors.

Coolidge's decision making is on display with his housing choices. He seemed to cast a practical eye and do what was necessary to get on with his life, sometimes quickly and sometimes after considerable thought. Successful networking, not luck, helped him along.

When other options were open, Coolidge made a statement every time that he decided to live and work in Northampton. Although sometimes he seemed to make decisions haphazardly, at other times he did careful research. In the summer of 1895, he wrote a letter to former Vermont Governor William Dillingham, then a Montpelier attorney, asking to read the law in his office. Because Dillingham was away on business, his positive reply did not reach Coolidge until after he had accepted the position at Hammond and Field in Northampton. It seems Coolidge gave himself some time to test his decision before replying to Dillingham on October 19, 1895 saying, in part, that the firm he had chosen was the best place for him outside of Vermont. If he had felt differently at this juncture, he could have negotiated with Hammond and Field and left for Vermont without losing face or for that matter, much in the way of time or money.

When he passed the bar in 1897, few knew that he was actively researching where to set up a law practice, as Hammond and Field did not add their 'graduates' to their office. After considering Lee, Massachusetts and various Vermont and New Hampshire locations, on August 26, 1897, he wrote to his father that the more he thought about his situation, the more he wanted to stay in Northampton. He reasoned that his expenses would be about the same as in a smaller place, but life would be more pleasant in this city.

Later in life, he made similar choices. While in 1929 the press speculated about what the president would do when he left office and where he would live, it appears that he and Grace were decisive about returning to the two-family on Massasoit Street. However, a year later when they realized that they had outgrown the duplex and needed a larger, more private space, they chose Northampton again when even the *Daily Hampshire Gazette* speculated that there were several other likely locations.

Coolidge's selection of places to live within the city seems to follow a similar pattern. Research was involved sometimes, and at other points, necessity and time constraints made the decision look unstudied. Rooming with the Lavakes at 162 King Street was a decision probably made with the help of his friend, Jim Lucey, the shoemaker. Necessity was an issue because he needed to start his study at Hammond and Field before the election season overwhelmed the attorneys. When Mrs. Lavake died in June 1896, he was faced with making another pressured choice, but he had met a genial clerk in a bookshop, and Rob Weir invited him to join him in rooming at John and Mary Lyman's house at 63 Center Street. Mrs. Lyman died in June 1897, and although it is possible that the two men stayed on with Mr. Lyman and his daughter, Carrie, in charge, it is not clear where the two men lived until August 1, 1897, when Rob Weir became the steward of Clarke School, a position that came with housing. Moving with Weir to Round Hill Road was probably a well-thought-out decision. To an aspiring Republican politician, the location in Ward 2 was attractive because it was that party's stronghold at that time. It is a sign that the two men got along well for Coolidge to follow him there. Since Weir was given the housing free, he might have let Coolidge have a bargain on the rent, another strong enticement.

After Coolidge married Grace in 1905, housing decisions are likely to have been made together. The fact that the couple did not have a place to live lined up before their wedding day is interesting. Could it be that the two young people were so in love that they thought everything would fall into place without much attention on their part or were they just disorganized? Had all Coolidge's energy been expended debating with his future mother-in-law about the wedding date? Their stay at the Norwood Hotel was short and given the establishment's financial status, they found something more permanent at just the right moment. They moved to a furnished house in their old neighborhood—close to Clarke School, and they saw the duplex at 21 Massasoit Street that would become their home in 1906. Nine months later they indeed moved there to one side of a two-family house. Its address was also in Ward 2, although Calvin never ran for another office where ward boundaries mattered. The Beeches also appears to be a planned move, an address they had known was for sale since their return from Washington. The crash in October 1929 may have meant that they got a bargain, but the custom of using the phrase "$1.00 and other good and valuable considerations" in deeds makes the actual price paid speculation.

After Coolidge died, the city wanted to dedicate a fitting memorial to him, and the close connection between people and their houses was again illustrated. In the spring of 1934, the city appointed a committee to gather and evaluate suggestions. Edmund Lampron, a Democratic member of the Common Council, received unanimous support for his proposal to appoint a committee of eleven to determine the nature of that tribute. Some of the names are familiar: Attorney Walter Stevens, Jim Lucey, Judge Henry Field, Attorney Ralph Hemenway, Dr. Frederic Plummer, and Mary Bailey.

The first idea came from Dr. John Allen, the Coolidge family dentist for twenty-five years and was reported in the *Gazette* three days after the committee was announced. He advised buying 21 Massasoit Street for a museum. Grace's friend and former neighbor, Therese Hills, seconded the idea, sure that there would always be interest in the house. Purchasing The Beeches for the same purpose was put forth in August of that year.

Before reporting its findings in December 1934, the committee met six times including one hearing at the high school to solicit public suggestions. The range of ideas was interesting—from a boulder to a riverside park to at least two bridges. The committee's final suggestion was to erect gates and put tablets and a statue in Main Street Park then rename it Calvin Coolidge Memorial Park. The idea was discarded, and the area between Memorial Hall and the Academy of Music is now known as Pulaski Park.

In 1939, a new bridge over the Connecticut River that bears his name (and some of the best art deco design elements in the valley) was opened and is still in use today. This suggestion was first made by the Northampton Municipal Employees Association because they felt that Coolidge himself would have appreciated a tribute that was necessary, useful, and enduring.

References

Albright, W. F. "Elihu Grant." *Bulletin of the American Schools of Oriental Research 88* (1942).

Bailey, Sidney P. "Remembering the Coolidges and the Beeches." July 5, 2001, manuscript in the collection of the Calvin Coolidge Presidential Library and Museum, Forbes Library, Northampton, Mass.

Butcher, Philip. *George W. Cable: The Northampton Years.* New York: Columbia University Press, 1959.

Catalog of Officers, Graduates and Non-Graduates 1875-1925 with Report of the Alumnae Association for 1924-1925. Northampton, Mass.: The Alumnae Association of Smith College, 1925.

Catalogue of Amherst College for the Year 1894-1895. Amherst, Mass.: Amherst College, 1894.

City Directories, Northampton and Easthampton, Mass. Northampton, Mass.: The Price and Lee Co., Compilers and Publishers, Gazette Printing Company, 1885-1950.

Cody, Jeffrey W. *Building in China: Henry K. Murphy's "Adaptive Architecture," 1914-1935.* Seattle: University of Washington Press, 2001.

Coolidge, Calvin. *The Autobiography of Calvin Coolidge.* New York: Cosmopolitan Book Corporation, 1929.

_____. Letters to Therese Christiansen Hills. Papers. Calvin Coolidge Presidential Library and Museum, Forbes Library, Northampton, Mass.

Coolidge, Grace. *Grace Coolidge An Autobiography.* Edited by Lawrence E. Wikander and Robert H. Ferrell. Worland, Wyo.: High Plains Publishing Company, Inc., 1992.

_____, ed. "The Real Calvin Coolidge: A First-Hand Story of His Life, Told by 50 People Who Knew Him Best and Edited with Comment by Grace Coolidge." *Good Housekeeping,* February-June 1935.

_____. Letters to Therese Christiansen Hills. Papers. Calvin Coolidge Presidential Library and Museum, Forbes Library, Northampton, Mass.

_____. Letter to Almy Chase Grant, June 1, 1928. Papers of Elihu Grant. Smith College Archives, Northampton, Mass.

Daily Hampshire Gazette, a newspaper established in 1786 in Northampton, Mass. It has had several names, including the *Hampshire Gazette* and after one merger, the longer and more cumbersome title, the *Hampshire Gazette and Northampton Courier.*

Fuess, Claude M. *Calvin Coolidge: The Man From Vermont.* Boston: Little, Brown and Company, 1940.

Grant, Dr. Elihu. "Mr. Coolidge as a Neighbor." *The Grant Game,* January-February 1924, New York: W. T. Grant Company. Reprint in Elihu Grant Papers. Smith College Archives, Northampton, Mass.

Grant, William T. and G. Lynn Sumner. *The Story of W. T. Grant and the Early Days of the Business He Founded.* New York: W. T. Grant Company, 1954.

Harrison, Joseph L. "Homes of Calvin Coolidge in Northampton." Papers. Calvin Coolidge Presidential Library and Museum, Forbes Library, Northampton, Mass., 1940.

Jewish Women's Archive, "JWAGertrudeWeil Excerpts from Letters from Gertrude Weil to her family."http://www.jwa.org/exhibits/wov/weil/gwlet112098EX.html (August 2, 2006).

Knab, Frederick. *Northampton of Today – 1902-1903.* Northampton, Mass.: Picturesque Publishing Company, 1902.

Lathem, Edward C., ed. *Meet Calvin Coolidge: The Man Behind the Myth.* Brattleboro, Vt.: The Stephen Greene Press, 1960.

_____, ed. *Your Son, Calvin Coolidge.* Montpelier, Vt.: Vermont Historical Society, 1968.

Logan, John A. and Mary Simmerson Cunningham Logan. *The Part Taken By Women in American History.* Wilmington, Del.: The Perry-Nalle Publishing Company, 1912.

Lyman, Clifford H., "Bridgman and Lyman's Bookstore 1797-1937." Papers. The Forbes Library, Northampton, Mass.

_____, "Reminiscences of Northampton 1882-1938." Papers. The Forbes Library, Northampton, Mass.

McAlester, Virginia and Lee. *A Field Guide to American Houses.* New York: Alfred A. Knopf, Inc., 1984.

McCoy, Donald R. *Calvin Coolidge: The Quiet President.* New York: The MacMillan Company, 1967.

MacCracken, Henry Noble. *The Hickory Limb.* New York: Charles Scribner's Sons, 1950.

_____, Papers. Smith College Archives, Box 4, Office of the President, Marion LeRoy Burton Series.

Montgomery, James. "Coolidge to His Shoemaker." *Personality*, Vol. 1 No. 1, (1927): 3-8.

Nagai, Isaburo, "The People's Institute of Northampton." Papers. W.E.B. Du Bois Library, University of Massachusetts Amherst, Special Collections and Archives, MS 26.

Northampton Historical Commission, Form B and National Register Nomination for 19-21 Massasoit Street. Calvin Coolidge Presidential Library and Museum, Forbes Library, Northampton, Mass.

Penner, The Reverend Albert J. Diaries. Private collection.

People's Institute of Northampton Home Culture Clubs, Minutes of Board Meetings. Papers. W.E.B. Du Bois Library, University of Massachusetts Amherst, Special Collections and Archives, MS 26.

Plummer, Frederic. *Boston Globe*. May 18-22, 24, 1930.

Ross, Ishbel. *Grace Coolidge and Her Era*. New York: Dodd, Mead & Company, 1962.

Seelye, Henrietta Chapin. Journal 1905-1909. Papers. Smith College Archives, Northampton, Mass.

Smith Alumnae Quarterly, Vol. 32 No. 2, (1941).

Smith College. *Report of the President, 1905-1906*. Smith College Archives, Northampton, Mass.

Sobel, Robert. *Coolidge: An American Enigma*. Washington, D.C.: Regnery Publishing, Inc., 1998.

Sorley, Lewis. *Thunderbolt: General Creighton Abrams and the Army of His Times*. New York: Simon & Schuster, 1992.

Time Magazine, September 17, 1928; February 18, 1929.

Wilson, Charles Reagan and William Ferris, eds. *Encyclopedia of Southern Culture*. Chapel Hill: University of North Carolina Press, 1989.

Wright, G. Ernest. "Elihu Grant." *Bulletin of the American Schools of Oriental Research 88* (1942).

Notes

Abbreviations

C Coolidge—Coolidge, Calvin. *The Autobiography of Calvin Coolidge.* New York: Cosmopolitan Book Corporation, 1929.

CCPLM—Calvin Coolidge Presidential Library and Museum, Forbes Library, Northampton, Massachusetts.

DHG—*Daily Hampshire Gazette*, a newspaper established in Northampton in 1786. It has had a number of names including, after one merger, the *Hampshire Gazette and Northampton Courier.*

Fuess—Fuess, Claude M. *Calvin Coolidge: The Man From Vermont.* Boston: Little, Brown and Company, 1940.

G Coolidge—Coolidge, Grace A. *Grace Coolidge An Autobiography.* Edited by Lawrence E. Wikander and Robert H. Ferrell. Worland, Wyo.: High Plains Publishing Company, Inc., 1992.

HCRDeeds—Hampshire County Registry of Deeds, Northampton, Massachusetts.

Lathem—Lathem, Edward C., editor. *Your Son, Calvin Coolidge.* Montpelier, Vt.: Vermont Historical Society, 1968.

Sobel—Sobel, Robert. *Coolidge: An American Enigma.* Washington, D.C.: Regnery Publishing, Inc., 1998.

Preface

On Calvin Coolidge's early life in Vermont, see C Coolidge, chapter one, "Childhood Scenes," and Fuess, chapter two, "Birth and Boyhood." My description of Plymouth, Vermont comes from Fuess, page 8 and from a personal visit to the village.

Joseph Leroy Harrison was the librarian of Forbes Library, Northampton, from 1912 to 1950. His long tenure had a major impact on the institution, particularly its special collections. In 1920, he began accumulating the historical items that form the basis for the CCPLM, some from the Coolidges themselves.

Chapter 1 Learning the Law, Turning to Politics

Calvin wrote a letter to his father dated October 1, 1895 about his first experiences in Northampton. See Lathem, page 76.

For the quote about the summer of 1895, see C Coolidge, page 71. His preference for law school is in a letter to his father in Lathem, May 3, 1895, page 68. Later he praised reading the law as opposed to law school; see C Coolidge, page 83. His first political foray is described by Fuess, page 81.

On the important cases of Hammond and Field, see Frederick Knab, *Northampton of Today–1902-1903*, Picturesque Publishing Company, Northampton, Mass., 1902, page 81.

For the quote that Hammond was the leader of the bar, see C Coolidge, page 72.

On joining the canoe club, see C Coolidge, page 76. That it was the Wish-Ton-Wish Club is revealed by Fuess, page 78.

Calvin's letter to his father written in Amherst about Maine politics is dated September 11, 1894 and is reprinted in Lathem, page 59. On Colonel Coolidge's political nature, see Fuess, page 16.

The letter to the editor defending the gold standard is reported by both C Coolidge, page 77, and Fuess, page 81.

Two Shoemakers

The Harrison manuscript, page 1, contains the basic information known about the house at 162 King Street and the family's reaction to their tenant, Calvin Coolidge.

The Lavakes' dates of death are recorded at the Northampton city clerk's office. Mr. Lavake and his ancestors had wills recorded at the Hampshire County Registry of Probate in the same city.

Coolidge's friendship with James Lucey, the shoemaker, was widely reported. The public became interested when the 'love' note, which is now in the collection of the CCPLM, was discovered. The quotes in this chapter are from James Montgomery's "Coolidge to His Shoemaker," *Personality*, Vol. I, No. I, November 1927, pages 5 and 6. That Lucey felt he had lost his best friend upon Coolidge's death is found in Sobel, page 414. Lucey's friends, Phil Gleason, the blacksmith, and John Dewey, the tavern keeper, were neighbors at 28 and 26 Park Street, respectively, during Coolidge's early years in the city. Today Park Street, Northampton is known as Trumbull Road. Gleason later moved to Bright Avenue. Ed Lynch boarded on State Street and later, Crescent. Coolidge's letter to Thomas Hammond was published in the *DHG*, April 22, 1926.

Information about the Hampton is found in the Harrison manuscript, page 2 and in the city directory cited in the text plus other directories until 1911. The *DHG* had reports on May 24, 1897, April 29, 1901 and November 2, 1904.

Parallel Lives on Center Street

Mr. Maynard purchased his house on May 2, 1884. See HCRDeeds, book 387, page 87. Mary Lyman bought 63 Center Street on July 29, 1884. See HCRDeeds, book 389, page 266. Mr. Lyman's obituary appears in the *DHG*,

May 16, 1905 while Mr. Maynard's obituary is in the May 18, 1905 edition.

Mabel Maynard's death date was found in the records of Northampton's city clerk. The living arrangements at 63 Center Street were described by Maynard and appear on page 1 of Harrison's manuscript.

The description of the red-haired girl is in Ishbel Ross, *Grace Coolidge and Her Era,* Dodd, Mead & Company, New York, 1962, page 10.

Information about the Lymans' Main Street business was found in the city directories and Knab, *Northampton of Today,* page 61.

The post-election quote is in the *Gazette and Courier,* a predecessor of the *DHG,* on March 4, 1884.

For the 2.75 beer story, see Donald McCoy, *Calvin Coolidge: The Quiet President,* The MacMillan Company, New York, 1967, page 81. See McCoy, page 303, for a discussion of Coolidge and Prohibition including information about the Secretary of the Treasury and Attorney General. Sobel, page 280, related Coolidge's comments on good and bad laws. The quote from Colonel Theodore Roosevelt was found in *Good Housekeeping,* February 1935, page 183.

The Deans of the Hampshire County Bar

Information about J. C. Hammond and Henry P. Field can be found in their obituaries and tributes to them published at the time of their deaths in the *DHG.* Hammond died April 21, 1926 and Field on September 30, 1937. Comments on the two men are in C Coolidge, pages 72 and 73. The inscription in Field's copy of Coolidge's autobiography was reported in an article about the judge's fifty years as an attorney in the *DHG,* April 18, 1933 and in the editorial of the *DHG,* October 1, 1937. The author verified the inscription by examining the original copy at the CCPLM.

Hammond's comment about Coolidge was reported in the *DHG,* April 22, 1926. The letter to Colonel Coolidge about Hammond's later comments is in Lathem, August 16, 1897, page 81. Field's posthumous description of Coolidge was reported in the *DHG,* January 7, 1933.

The names of the attorneys admitted to the bar on July 2, 1897 were reported in the *DHG,* June 30, 1897 and confirmed by the Supreme Judicial Court of the Commonwealth of Massachusetts in 2008. Further information about the young Northampton lawyers at the turn of the last century was found in Knab, *Northampton of Today,* pages 81 and 82.

Coolidge's comments about Ernest Hardy are found in a letter to his father in Lathem, August 26, 1897, page 83. Coolidge's comments about the local bar are found in C Coolidge, page 85.

162 King Street

Charles Lavake was granted the property on August 23, 1872 by his brother-in-law and sister, Sherwood and Mary Ann Lavake Goodwin. See HCRDeeds, book 297, page 65. The parcel was acquired by Charles Lavake and Mary Ann Goodwin from their grandfather, Isaac Tower. The sale by Charles Lavake's heirs to John Moriarty is recorded in HCRDeeds, book 528, page 23, and the sale by the Northampton Cooooperative Bank to Bridget Moriarty is in book 610, page 257. The conversation with the present owner of 12-16 Carpenter Avenue took place in the spring of 2007.

63 Center Street

For ownership history, see HCRDeeds, book 389, page 266; book 657, page 473; and book 1120, page 373.

Chapter 2   Eight More Years a Bachelor

Mr. Connor's educational background is in Knab, *Northampton of Today*, page 82. Fuess, page 85 suggests the principle of rotation for the city solicitor's job.

The Cupid at Clark School

Weir's birth was found on Ancestry.com. *Ontario, Canada Births, 1869-1909* [database on-line]. Provo, Utah: The Generations Network, Inc. The Weirs' move to Tennessee was documented with information from the 1880 U.S. Census.

Moving North

The description of the Moffat family, especially their relation to characters in the book *John March, Southerner,* came from Philip Butcher, *George W. Cable: The Northampton Years*, New York, Columbia University Press, 1959, page 135.

The history and philosophy of the Home Culture Clubs was found in Philip Butcher, *George W. Cable: The Northampton Years;* in John Logan and Mary Logan, *The Part Taken By Women in American History*, Wilmington, Del.: The Perry-Nalle Publishing Company, 1912, pages 393-395; and in the *New York Times,* May 24, 1896 reprinted from the *Springfield (*Mass.*) Republican.*

The description of Smith College students' involvement with the clubs is found in Knab, *Northampton of Today,* page 49 and Isaburo Nagai, "The People's Institute of Northampton," manuscript in W.E.B. Du Bois Library, University of Massachusetts Amherst, Special Collections and Archives, MS 26. Gertrude

Weil, Smith College, Class of 1901, was considering starting an organization based on the Home Culture Clubs model when she returned home to North Carolina. She wrote the first letter quoted in October 1898 and the second one on November 20, 1898. She was honored as a "Woman of Valor" by the Jewish Women's Archives in 2002.

Adelene Moffat talked with Philip Butcher in New York City in the 1950s. His book is the source of the description of events leading to Moffat's resignation from the clubs and its aftermath. For those readers with a greater interest in local history, a summary, based on the book and articles in the *DHG* and the *Herald* in 1907 follows:

In a letter to Adelene Moffat in early March 1907, George W. Cable noted that the clubs' finances were in the red and stated that reducing the payroll was the only way to achieve real savings. "Yet we are in constant need for more clerical work rather than less…our administrative work must be done by one secretary and that he must be a man" (Butcher, page 213). She felt that her only recourse was to resign. Her friend and clubs' board member, Frank Lyman, conveyed her resignation to the board and submitted his own at the same time. A special meeting of the board of directors was held on March 18, 1907 when her resignation was accepted by a resolution that also praised her work. The secretary of the board, Calvin Coolidge, was absent. (Butcher, page 197.) The board unanimously voted to tell Mr. Lyman that his resignation had been received with regret and to ask him to reconsider. The Home Culture Clubs had a six-person board – Coolidge, the secretary, and Frank Lyman were absent – so voting were Cable, Dr. John A. Houston, Smith College President L. Clark Seelye, and A. Lyman Williston. Lyman would be a great loss to the organization because besides Cable, he and his sister were the major sources of financial support.

On March 20, 1907, the *Gazette* printed the board's resolution and added this tribute to Moffat: "…for years during the development of the work, she was its chief worker and a large share of its success and growth is directly due to her." Buried in a list of city items on another page of the same edition was this tribute from her friends: "There were only a few scattered clubs, with but two small rooms on the upper floor over McCallum's for headquarters when she became associated with the movement. She has worked early and late, faithfully and industriously, and most successfully for the clubs until their work has reached a proportion that the friends did not dream of fifteen years ago" (*DHG*, March 20, 1907, pages 3 and 5). The *Daily Herald* printed a story and both continued their coverage in ensuing days because the matter was not over.

The Women's Council, an advisory group, met on April 3 for its regular meeting, and Cable was present. With an unusually large attendance, the group proposed a resolution praising Moffat and petitioning the board to persuade her to remain with the clubs. The *Daily Herald* printed the petition the next day and followed on April 5 with an editorial suggesting that the public had great sympathy for Moffat and announcing clearly that her resignation was not voluntary. The *Herald* raised concerns about the management style and the financial dealings of the clubs. Although the *Herald* did not report it, Moffat's salary was low and often left unpaid. In a small item almost buried and unnoticeable, a *Gazette* writer on April 6 cautioned people about dealing in rumor and said that during the first years Cable had put in thousands of his own money and took time from his own work "when he was at his best." Board members Coolidge and Williston wrote separately to Cable advising him that the resignation should be left standing despite the Women's Council and media concerns.

On May 13, the board met again to accept Lyman's resignation and thank him for his more than generous financial support. According to Coolidge's minutes, the board considered the Women's Council petition and thought it was "inexpedient in view of all the circumstances to reconsider our action with reference to Miss Moffat's resignation." They left it to the finance committee to deal with Adelene Moffat's claim for back salary. She hired Attorney John C. Hammond, Coolidge's mentor and an original Home Culture Clubs board member. The board appointed Coolidge as their representative to settle the matter. Her claim was settled for $1,000 in June 1908 with money the board borrowed from Northampton Institution for Savings. (Butcher, page 239.)

Clifford Lyman told of the Weir brothers' association with the bookstore in his manuscript, "Bridgman and Lyman Bookstore, 1797-1937," page 2. Lyman related the California stationery connections in another manuscript, "Reminiscences of Northampton, 1882-1938," page 11. Both are housed in the Hampshire Room of the Forbes Library, Northampton.

Rob Weir's trip to Tennessee in 1897 was mentioned as a 'city item' in the *DHG*, July 2, 1897. The information about the makeup of the Weir household in 1900 is from the U.S. Census.

Shared Interests

A search of the city directories from 1899 to 1920 shows no other elections to the city council except those mentioned. Weir served as an elector under the will of Oliver Smith in 1905 and 1906 according to the same directories.

Lyman's 'Wit and Wisdom' columns appeared in the *DHG,* January 9 and September 28, 1936. Judge Field's anecdote is reported in the latter article.

The Introduction

For the description of Robert Weir, see Fuess, page 87. Grace Coolidge tells of her meeting and first date with Calvin in G Coolidge, pages 30 and 31. Grace related the 'macaroon' incident on page 205 of *Good Housekeeping,* June 1935. The president's tribute to his wife is in C Coolidge, page 93.

Losing Touch

The Weir family's sojourn in California was documented by the U.S. Censuses of 1910, 1920 and 1930. Their deaths are on Ancestry.com, California Death Index, 1940-1997.

Weir's associations with Bouchard and Day are related by Clifford Lyman in the *DHG,* January 9, 1936 and September 28, 1936. The obituary in the *Sacramento Bee,* reprinted in the *DHG,* September 15, 1936, states that Weir lived in Sacramento seven years. The quote about Rob's tendency to get the 'blues' is from Lyman's tribute printed in the *DHG,* September 15, 1936.

George Washington Cable

Cable is easily researched online because his work is mentioned in many college courses on southern writers, and he is considered the first modern southern author. A brief biography is found in Charles Wilson and William Ferris, editors, *Encyclopedia of the South,* Chapel Hill: University of North Carolina Press, 1989. Other material for this sidebar came from Butcher, *George W. Cable: The Northampton Years,* especially page 197 where it is reported that Cable told Harry B. Taplin, a Home Culture Clubs employee, to watch Coolidge for future greatness.

Richard Rahar

Coolidge remembers eating at Rahar's Inn in his autobiography, page 92. Rahar's family was found in the U.S. Census of 1880 and the city directories. His travel history is in ships' passenger lists available on Ancestry.com. Mr. Rahar's memories were included in the February 1935 edition of *Good Housekeeping,* page 188 as is the story about the finger bowl/lemon soup written by Grace Coolidge.

Chapter 3 Newlywed

Grace's story about cutting the honeymoon short was found in Edward Latham, editor, *Meet Calvin Coolidge: the Man Behind the Myth,* The Stephen Greene Press, Brattleboro, Vt., 1960, page 63. Fuess's story about the 1905 Northampton school committee race is found on page 90. Information on the opening of the Norwood is in a *DHG* article published April 11, 1905. Fuess wrote that the stay at the Norwood was three weeks on page 89. Grace Coolidge wrote her version in G Coolidge, page 35.

Renting a Library of Classics

Brady's sick leave is confirmed in the Smith College *Report of the President, 1905-1906.* The date Professor and Mrs. Brady departed for Florida is recorded in the journal of Henrietta Chapin Seelye, wife of the first president of Smith College, on November 3, 1905. Personal information about Professor Brady was gleaned from his obituary in the *Smith Alumnae Quarterly,* February 1941 (Vol. 32 No. 2), page 109.

Coolidge talked about his love of translating the classics in C Coolidge, page 73. Grace describes her husband's library and reading habits in *Good Housekeeping,* June 1935, page 207.

The Norwood, 31 Bridge Street

The *Springfield Republican* and the *DHG* described the money spent and the configuration of the Norwood on December 31, 1892 and September 3, 1892, respectively. A new proprietor was announced in the *DHG,* December 13, 1900. Colonel Keeler and his renovations were discussed in the *DHG,* April 11, 1905, and the closing was announced in the October 26, 1905 edition. That it would become a hospital was reported in the *DHG,* September 19, 1907. Grace describes the separation of the buildings and the subsequent uses in Lathem, *Meet Calvin Coolidge,* page 63. It was also written about in the *DHG,* April 5, 1910.

5 Crescent Street

Shingle style homes are described in Virginia and Lee McAlester, *A Field Guide to American Houses,* New York: Alfred A. Knopf, Inc., 1984, pages 289-290. Today's house size is from the records of the Northampton assessors.

The cost of building houses on Crescent Street was in the *Springfield Republican,* December 31, 1892. For sales of property, see HCRDeeds, book 418, page 34; book 464, page 21; book 704, page 435; and book 747, page 519.

Chapter 4 The Settled Life

The Neighbors Who Were So Kind

Grace told of her love for the house on Massasoit Street in G Coolidge, page 104. The president discussed moving to the property and his reluctance to move out of this house in C Coolidge, page 95. He told how he was named in the same book, page 7.

The list of furnishings at 21 Massasoit Street is from Ross, *Grace Coolidge and Her Era,* pages 25 and 26 and from studying photographs of the rooms in the collection of the CCPLM.

The telegram to Gompers is quoted in full in Fuess, page 226. Coolidge's 'I do not choose to run' statement is reproduced in Fuess, page 393.

Elihu Grant described the neighborhood on page 1 of his article, "Mr. Coolidge as a Neighbor," *The Grant Game,* January-February 1924, New York: W. T. Grant Company. Grace Coolidge described her sons' friends in G Coolidge, page 44. Coolidge teaching his neighbor to swing a scythe was reported by Grant on page 3 of "Mr. Coolidge as a Neighbor." W. T. Grant proudly described his brother on page 7 of *The Story of W. T. Grant and the Early Days of the Business He Founded,* W. T. Grant Company, 1954. A brief biography of Professor Grant was found in the *Bulletin of the American Schools of Oriental Research,* No. 88, December 1942, Baltimore, Md., page 2 in an article by G. Ernest Wright. His treatment of his Arab workers was discussed in the same journal on page 3 in an observation by W. F. Albright. W. T. Grant's tale of advice from Coolidge was on page 40 of *The Story of W. T. Grant.* Elihu Grant described Coolidge's personality on pages 1 and 2 and his quietness on page 3 of "Mr. Coolidge as a Neighbor."

Plummer's reports of the gardening at 21 Massasoit Street are in the *Boston Globe,* May 19, 1930. The six articles in the *Globe* are the source for all of Plummer's comments. They were published Sunday-Thursday, May 18-May 24, 1930 and Saturday, May 26, 1930. The story of the spruce trees is from Sidney P. Bailey, "Remembering the Coolidges and the Beeches," July 5, 2001, a manuscript in the collection of the CCPLM. The Washington party in early 1929 was reported in *Time* magazine, February 18, 1929. Hemenway's story is reprinted in Lathem, *Meet Calvin Coolidge,* page 171.

The Reverend Penner kept diaries his entire life and in retirement wrote a summary of many of the years. His tale of Coolidge's note to Clifford Lyman, then in Penner's possession, was found in the summary of his 1933 diary.

Information about Dr. Frederic Plummer's background and his appointment as principal of the high school was reported in the *DHG,* May 4, 1918. His retirement was found in the *DHG,* June 23, 1937 in an article that included the fact that he encouraged young men to attend the service academies. His son, Thomas Plummer, was appointed to West Point according to the *DHG,* July 15, 1921 and graduated in 1926 as reported in the *DHG,* June 12, 1926.

For more information about General Creighton Abrams's youth, see Lewis Sorley, *Thunderbolt: General Creighton Abrams and the Army of His Times,* Simon & Schuster, New York, 1992, page 16.

The note to Almy Chase Grant from Grace Coolidge was dated June 1, 1928 and is in the Smith College Archives, Northampton.

Mrs. Coolidge's story about Professor Grant's visit is in *Good Housekeeping,* June 1935, page 201. Plummer told of his family's affection for Mrs. Goodhue in the *Boston Globe,* May 24, 1930. For a description of Mrs. Goodhue, see her obituary in the *DHG,* October 25, 1929. The "Pork and Beans" comment was reported by Plummer in the *Boston Globe,* May 24, 1930. Mrs. Reckahn's place in the household is told by Fuess, page 91.

Therese Hills's birthplace is noted in her obituary in the *DHG,* December 28, 1970. A typewritten letter from the president to Mrs. Hills mentioning the chocolates was dated January 26, 1929. A handwritten letter to Mrs. Hills from Grace with regard to the crates to be stored at her house was postmarked February 27, 1929. The two letters cited from the Coolidge correspondence to Therese Hills is in the collection of the CCPLM.

The entire story of John Coolidge's twenty-second birthday was related in *Time* magazine, September 17, 1928.

Typewritten letters from Calvin Coolidge to Therese Hills about the rug are dated January 26 and 29, 1929 and are in the collection of the CCPLM. Plummer revealed his traffic count in the *Boston Globe,* May 19, 1930.

19-21 Massasoit Street

The National Register nomination and the Form B for the property are in the collection of the CCPLM. The house was listed on the National Register on December 12, 1976. Plummer's use of the third floor was reported in the *Boston Globe,* May 19, 1930. The Tea Room that operated at 21 Massasoit Street for a time was discussed in the *DHG,* August 21, 1936.

Chapter 5 The Best Home for the Coolidges

Building the Beeches

Copies of the contract between MacCracken and Huxley plus the accounts and estimates are in the collection of the CCPLM, gifts of Daisy Mathias and Bob Nelson, former owners of The Beeches. The MacCrackens' life in Northampton and their move to Vassar is in Henry MacCracken's memoir, *The Hickory Limb*, Charles Scribner's Sons, New York, 1950. Letters from MacCracken to Burton are dated October 16, 1913 and December 26, 1913 and are in the Smith College Archives, box 4, Office of the President, Marion LeRoy Burton Series. The story about their train travel and the quote about the wrong side of town are in MacCracken, page 10.

The purchases of the two parcels of land in 1914 are recorded in the HCRDeeds, book 698, page 433 and book 750, page 277. The description of the plans for the property was in the *DHG*, January 19, 1914. The progress or lack thereof on the building is in MacCracken's memoir, *The Hickory Limb*. His obituary was printed in the *New York Times*, May 8, 1970.

Information about the architects and the firm's China connection was found in Jeffrey W. Cody, *Building in China: Henry K. Murphy's "Adaptive Architecture," 1914-1935,* University of Washington Press, Seattle, 2001 and on a Yale website, www.library.yale.edu/div/colleges/descriptions.htm.

Frank Huxley's obituary appeared in the *DHG*, June 18, 1928. MacCracken explained the original name for the house, The Tryst, on page 10 of *The Hickory Limb*. The home as it was when the Coolidges purchased it was described by the *DHG*, April 1 and 5, 1930. The quote about the paths and wading pool is from MacCracken, page 13.

Sidney P. Bailey's memories of The Beeches when his family owned it, and the quote about his mother's annoyance about the bells and elevator use, were found in "Remembering the Coolidges and the Beeches," July 5, 2001, a manuscript in the collection of the CCPLM. The Comeys' mortgage and mortgage release are in the HCRDeeds, book 750, page 281 and book 815, page 352.

A Modest Place

Coolidge's announcement about purchasing The Beeches, the newspaper's reaction, and Mrs. Comey's tour for reporters were reported in the *DHG*, April 1, 2 and 5, 1930 respectively. The number of reporters on the tour was reported in *Time* magazine, April 14, 1930. Morris Comey's obituary was printed in the *DHG*, April 27, 1925.

The actual move by the Coolidges was chronicled in the *DHG*, May 14, 16 and 19, 1930. The former president's quip about it not being easy to get out of the White House was in *Time* magazine, February 25, 1929. The quote from the *DHG* about the Coolidges intention to call Northampton home is from the April 2, 1930 edition.

Coolidge's retirement activities are explained by Fuess, page 449. While his death was probably reported by every newspaper in the land, Fuess, page 463, summarizes the circumstances. His daily routine was described by Frederic Plummer and in numerous media accounts of his death including the *New York Times*, January 6, 1933.

Stories about the Baileys were told by their son, Sidney P. Bailey in "Remembering the Coolidges and the Beeches." Mrs. Adams's homes in Northampton and North Carolina and Grace's Road Forks on Ward Avenue were designed by noted local architect Karl Putnam. The *New York Times*, June 10, 1919, reported Coolidge's feelings about women's suffrage as a result of a statement to the press upon sending the amendment to the Massachusetts legislature.

Conclusion

The third article in Frederic Plummer's series of six for the *Boston Globe* published May 20, 1930 reveals his frustrations with his 'silent neighbor'. However, in his article published May 18, 1930, also in the *Globe*, Plummer states that he could not imagine easier neighbors under these circumstances.

For letters from Coolidge to former Vermont Governor Dillingham, see Fuess, pages 73 and 74. For letter to Colonel Coolidge from Calvin about a place to practice law, see Lathem, August 26, 1897. Alternatives to Northampton as a place to live after the presidency are found in the *DHG*, April 2, 1930.

The work of the city's committee to determine the memorial to Coolidge was reported throughout 1934, beginning with the report of its appointment on May 14, 1934 in the *DHG*. Edmund Lampron, who suggested creating the committee, was added to its roster, according to the *DHG*, May 23, 1934. The suggestion that the half house become a museum was discussed in the *DHG* on May 17 and 18, 1934. Other *DHG* editions to read on this topic are May 23, June 1 and 2, July 5, August 7 and December 21, 1934. The information from the *DHG* about the bridge as a memorial was published on May 23, 1934.

About the Author

Susan Well is a writer with a passion for history, especially that of Northampton, Massachusetts and its homes and people. Having lived there since 1973, she satisfied her interest in houses by working as a Realtor and later, a real estate appraiser. She chaired Northampton's Historical Commission and co-chaired the city's 350th Anniversary Committee. Well graduated from Cornell University in 1968, a year presidential politics took a number of fateful, even deadly, turns. She earned a master's degree from Springfield (Mass.) College and now enjoys retirement with her husband, Arnie.